MUDRAS
for PTSD
8 WEEK GUIDEBOOK

RELEASE and RECODE
Your AURA INJURY

SABRINA MESKO

Author of International Bestseller HEALING MUDRAS

By Sabrina Mesko

HEALING MUDRAS
Yoga for Your Hands
Random House - Original edition
Mudra Hands Publishing - New Edition

POWER MUDRAS
Yoga Hand Postures for Women
Random House - Original edition
Mudra Hands Publishing - New Edition

MUDRA - Gestures of POWER
DVD - Sounds True

CHAKRA MUDRAS DVD set
HAND YOGA for Vitality, Creativity and Success
HAND YOGA for Concentration, Love and Longevity

HEALING MUDRAS - New Edition in full color:
Healing Mudras I. ~ For Your Body
Healing Mudras II. ~ For Your Mind
Healing Mudras III. ~ For Your Soul

MUDRA THERAPY
Hand Yoga for Pain Management and Conquering Illness

YOGA MIND
45 Meditations for Inner Peace, Prosperity and Protection

MUDRAS for ASTROLOGICAL SIGNS
Volumes I. ~ XII.
**MUDRAS for ARIES, TAURUS, GEMINI, CANCER, LEO, VIRGO,
LIBRA, SCORPIO, SAGITTARIUS, CAPRICORN, AQUARIUS, PISCES**
12 Book Series

LOVE MUDRAS
Hand Yoga for Two

MUDRAS AND CRYSTALS
The Alchemy of Energy Protection

THE HOLISTIC CAREGIVER
A Guidebook for at-home care in late stage of Alzheimer's and dementia

YOUR SPIRITUAL PURPOSE
Intentions and Choices

The **Holistic Mudra Series**

MUDRAS
for PTSD
8 WEEK GUIDEBOOK

RELEASE and RECODE Your AURA INJURY

SABRINA MESKO

Author of International Bestseller HEALING MUDRAS

Book Two

The material contained in this book has been written for informational
purposes and is not intended as a substitute for medical advice,
nor is it intended to diagnose, treat, cure, or prevent disease.
If you have a medical issue or illness, consult a qualified physician.

A MUDRA Hands™ Book

Published by Mudra Hands Publishing
an Imprint of

ARNICA PRESS
www.ArnicaPress.com

Copyright © 2018, 2022 Sabrina Mesko

Written by Sabrina Mesko
Illustrations by Kiar Mesko
Author Photo by Mara
On the Cover:
MUDRA for Closing off Your Aura

Manufactured in the United States of America
ISBN: 978-1-955354-31-8

To All Who Suffer,
May You Heal and Suffer No More,

To All Who Long for Love,
May Divine Love Replenish Your Heart,

To All who are Here to Uplift Humanity,
May You be Supported, Protected and Victorious…

THE MUDRA PRACTICE IS A COMPLIMENTARY HEALING TECHNIQUE,
THAT OFFERS FAST AND EFFECTIVE POSITIVE RESULTS.

MUDRAS WORK HARMONIOUSLY WITH OTHER TRADITIONAL,
ALTERNATIVE AND COMPLEMENTARY HEALING PROTOCOLS.

THEY HELP RESTORE DEPLETED SUBTLE ENERGY STATES
AND OPTIMIZE THE PRACTITIONER'S
OVERALL STATE OF WELLNESS.

TABLE OF CONTENTS

INTRODUCTION

W elcome to a deeply healing journey! Your peek into the mirror of truth to examine your innermost vulnerabilities is mighty courageous. It will greatly improve and change your life in most profound ways.

Why? Because your first step to eliminate anything that stands in your way is to see it, acknowledge it, recognize it, and face it. Fearlessly, directly and with masterful discernment. There is no proper measuring formula to assess trauma. For someone, a seemingly small event will prove to be life-changing, for another, their tolerance can sustain much more. The level of trauma for two individuals that experience the same dramatic event, may be completely different. Trauma is an individual experience, as unique as are you. But no matter what kind of injury you've endured, it can be overcome and even empowering.

The main mission of this book is to help you conquer, heal, and release your individual PTSD. Know in your body, heart and mind, that you shall heal your wounds and thrive. Yes, you will thrive.

However, since every and each one of us makes up the whole of society we live in, a multi-layered healing process is required. We begin with ourselves, and we successfully complete the mission for us all.

We need to understand, recognize and help remedy the level of collective PTSD we are experiencing at this very moment. It certainly seems that the challenging global dynamics shall continue to be present in our near future. This requires a strong physical, mental and emotional resilience while living an optimally healthy lifestyle. It takes a conscious effort.

One could argue that the world history always presented traumatic events and caused humanity a certain level of collective PTSD. This is true, since trauma is unfortunately a part of human life. Just going back in time for the last one-hundred years, easily proves this point. Reflecting back even further through thousands of years of our history, we realize that ongoing conflicts and human suffering was endured by all our ancestors.

But perhaps recent struggles are magnified for specific reasons. For starters, there are more of us in the world than ever before. Our world is overcrowded and therefore conflict and unrest are magnified. Adding to the stress factors are the addictive technology and the obvious immediacy of news, that travels around the globe with lightning speed. We are living in an age of escalated and unprecedented levels of information and misinformation overload.

You may live in a part of the world that seems peaceful, yet the news will inform you of a tragedy on the other side of the globe. This may trigger in you an intense PTSD reaction. Witnessing suffering; whether it be human, in animal kingdom or general nature itself, can cause and dramatically increase deeply stressful memories in our psyche.

Subtle frequencies travel with lightning speed and current technology simultaneously informs the entire world of a dramatic event. Therefore magnified unharmonious, negative frequencies of fear, anger and conflict can envelop large populations all at once! This only escalates the negative vibrations and creates a disruptive resonance effect even in people that are simply physically present, but otherwise not personally engaged in a specific conflict.

In other words, if everyone around you is experiencing an upset, you are not immune to that disruptive energy wave. The power of disturbing frequency will affect your body, mind, thinking ability and emotional state. A powerful frequency will reverberate with such force, that it will affect everyone and everything within its reach. You are not immune to your environment, it can and will overpower you.

Your being will partake in a mass stressful or traumatic event, and you won't be able to help it. This will remain in your cellular memory and create a strong PTSD imprint. Natural disasters can reawaken memories of ancient traumatic experiences that you carry within and may have never witnessed in this life. And yet, on some distant level of your psyche, you remember an embedded sense of unease, unrest, distress and seemingly unfounded fear.

PTSD is a complex multi-layered condition that requires a thorough spiritual assessment and understanding of yourself. This is why the message and self-care tools in this book are more timely than ever. Self-observation and understanding your inner mysteries will help unravel and disassemble your vulnerabilities and transform them into your most valuable asset – inner wisdom.

PTSD is your teacher. It is a map to your inner world that longs and demands to be understood, and requires your dedicated attention. Patience, self-discovery and disciplined practice of Mudras will help cleanse any subtle energy congestion, so you can function at your optimal capacity. Mudras are your tools for recovery and thriving.

Only disciplined regular maintenance of your own healthy frequency field can protect and balance your inner makings. The times we live in demand a different kind of attention and care of our delicate beings. This is your required maintenance for the impending future we are all facing. It will help you heal any residuals of past PTSD and manage the collective PTSD that is ongoing and requires continuous care.

Now you have made this step and with regular daily practice, your power and inner strength will be noticeably growing, while the obstacles will keep on shrinking. We fear the unknown, what we can't see or understand. But once we identify the source and challenge itself, it suddenly becomes quite manageable, smaller, and a lot less obstructive.

Rest assured, this is going to be an enjoyable and pleasant journey, despite the intense topic. Your life's path that brought you to this moment was perhaps a bit unkind, a measure too harsh, or even very difficult, but now you've landed in a safe and nurturing oasis. Your eight-week journey will create a gentle healing space, a soft environment, where you can exhale, and leave all your worries behind. With inner calm and wisdom, you'll be able to observe and explore the seemingly unimportant past events, that are quite essential in understanding what influences your present or perhaps your entire future life.

The truth is, nothing is unimportant, everything matters. Above all, you and your health and happiness are most important. These past traumatic events may have been unusually tough, extra demanding, or simply did not offer you the support you needed. If you went through anything that was frightening, unpleasant, disturbing, or extremely difficult, you deserve more sweetness, kindness, compassion, and unconditional, supportive love in your life. You need a safe haven to have an opportunity to catch up, repair, heal, reassess and reestablish anything that you choose to.

Your dreams are still alive. It's time to find them again. It is entirely up to you what you decide to eliminate or shift in your life, as a result of this journey. Your future lies in your hands. You will know what's right, you will discern what's important, and you will consciously select a new, happy, empowered, wise, and most nurturing path to heal old wounds and move forward with enthusiasm, optimism and excitement for all the beautiful things that lie ahead.

It is my honor to light up your path out of the labyrinth of old anguish, and help you rediscover your way back to your heart. Because the most important experience in life is love. All roads of healing lead thru the gateway of efficient self-love, and the ability to receive and give love to another. This is the final realization, no matter how thorny the path. And now, your sacred space of healing awaits.

Endless Blessings and Love, my Spiritual Voyager...

Sabrina

HOW TO USE THIS BOOK

Your journey requires eight weeks of dedicated daily practice. A 30-minute daily routine includes a 10 minute Mudra practice, followed by a 5 minute meditation in stillness and concludes with 15 minutes of Inner Reflection Q&A journaling.

Each week read the chapter and reflect on new information. It may bring up some deep realizations and new discoveries that will help you understand and release unwanted thinking patterns that you carry within. Practice the Mudras every day and write your self-reflective thoughts and answers to the Questions in your Journal Workspace. You will find a new weekly affirmation that will help recreate new thinking patterns as you move forward.

There will be days where you won't feel like writing, and other days you will write up a storm. Everything marks a positive progress forward, since we are all different and require a self-healing process perfectly adapted to our individual needs. Time is not important, your inner transformation is what you are after. Trust your body's natural process, be patient, kind and compassionate with yourself. Commit to the process and you will make great progress.

At the conclusion of this journey, you will consciously shift your mindset and clear any clusters of subtle energy congestion. Your Aura will reenergize and your frequency shall ascend. This purifying effect will help you release any old trauma and replace it with a new, empowering, balancing and stabilizing healthy subtle-energy code.

You are in charge, your healing has begun, and your brilliant future is in your hands. I shall stand with you and support you through this empowering process as you experience a significant positive shift. You are on your way.

Reclaim your life with a new inner-conversation imprint:

I AM FREE, CAPABLE AND LOVED.
I AM FEARLESS, COURAGEOUS, CONFIDENT AND JOYFUL.
I AM GRATEFUL FOR ALL EXPERIENCES, PAST, PRESENT AND FUTURE.
THEY ARE MY GREATEST TREASURE.
I AM WHO I CHOSE TO BE.

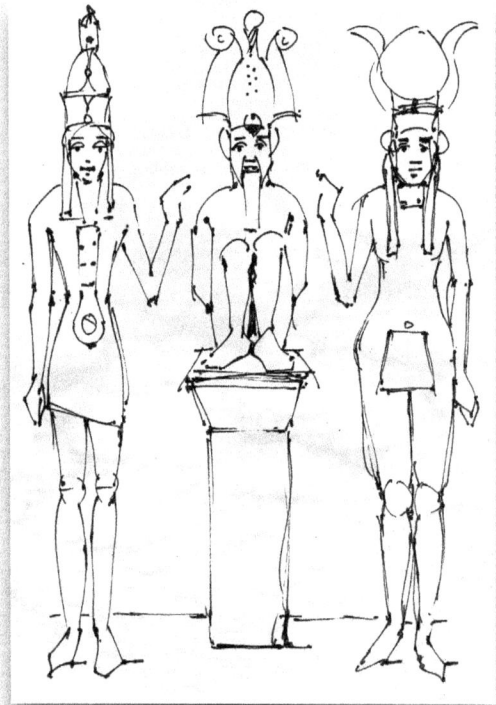

I. ABOUT MUDRAS

MUDRAS IN ANCIENT TIMES

Mudras originated in ancient Egypt over 5000 years ago and were used by High Priests and Priestesses in sacred healing rituals. Mudras seem quite easy to do, but are immensely powerful and effective when practiced correctly and with precision. There are countless examples of Mudras and hand gestures in iconic figures, sculptures and depictions from all continents of the world. Mudras are truly universal and can be found in every culture on Earth. In addition to advanced work with Mudras, the Priests and Priestesses of Ancient Egypt used numerous other sensory healing modalities such as crystals, advanced healing sound frequencies, color therapy and aromatherapy. I have written about the ancient healing Mudra techniques combined with various modalities in my *Holistic Mudra Book Series* and online mentorships. However, in this book, I share with you the specific transformative effects of Mudras for conquering PTSD.

WHAT ARE MUDRAS?

Mudras are sacred ancient healing hand gestures that use various intricate positions of fingers, hands, and arms. They carry very specific power activating formulas and can be used with ease, accuracy and assured success. Mudras are clear, simple, yet inexplicably powerful tools for self-healing and improving your overall physical, mental, and emotional state of well-being while magnifying your spiritual attunement. They are ancient codes to help you recharge, redirect, and reconfigure your subtle energy patterns.

How do Mudras Work?

From an energy anatomy perspective, Mudras work with precision of hand and finger placement. Our fingertips are connected to countless subtle energy currents – Nadis, that affect our entire physical, mental, emotional and energy body. Mudras are very easy to do, and can be practiced by anyone who can move their fingers, arms and hands. Simply by joining your fingertips in specific combinations, you are directly affecting, opening, cleansing, recharging and reactivating your subtle energy currents and Chakra centers. Proper Mudra hand placement is of utmost importance, specifically in relation to your body. A Mudra held above your head will affect you differently than the same Mudra positioned in your lap. Without following these very particular hand and body related placement descriptions, Mudra practice is incomplete and often ineffective. In addition, Mudras have to be practiced with proper breathing techniques to help facilitate and expedite the healing process and the subtle energy movement. Mudras are excellent for unblocking and eliminating congested energy clusters within your subtle body.

Aura, Chakras and Nadis

Your Aura is a highly perceptive yet invisible subtle energy field and sensory engine that is acutely sensitive to outside stimuli of your immediate environment. Along your spine are seven powerful energy centers, called Chakras. In their optimal state, they are spinning in a clockwise direction. These dynamic vortexes of energy affect every aspect of a specific physical region. They affect your physical health as well as mental and emotional disposition. In addition, your Aura contains 72.000 invisible energy currents called Nadis, running through your body, like subtle energy "veins". They are an intricate part of your highly sophisticated energy field and determine your general state of wellbeing.

In addition to the seven main Chakras, there are also smaller Chakras in the palms of your hands and soles of your feet. Usually the right hand is on the receiving end of subtle energy, while the left hand is naturally of more giving nature, since it is closer to your heart. The right side of your body is under the influence of the Sun, while the left side is under the influence of the Moon. As a result, the right hand affects one's mental and logical perception and is reflection of your masculine nature, while the left hand expresses your intuitive, emotional, feminine side. This placement is part of each person's subtle energy field. The ability of giving and receiving subtle energy can vary depending on the individual.

A highly sensory aware and intuitive person may be able to use both hands for intentional subtle energy transmitting, sharing, scanning, reading, healing, as well as receiving.

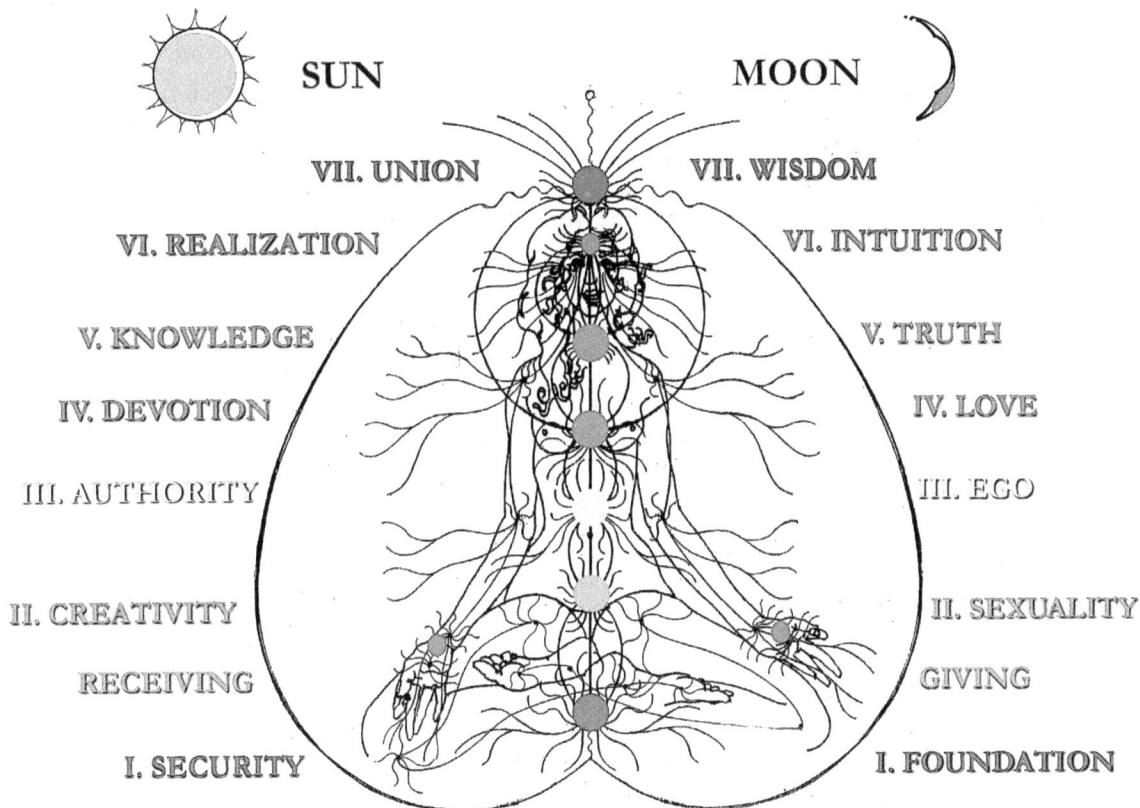

SUN   MOON

VII. UNION   VII. WISDOM

VI. REALIZATION   VI. INTUITION

V. KNOWLEDGE   V. TRUTH

IV. DEVOTION   IV. LOVE

III. AUTHORITY   III. EGO

II. CREATIVITY   II. SEXUALITY

RECEIVING   GIVING

I. SECURITY   I. FOUNDATION

HEALING BREATH

Another very important aspect of Mudra practice is proper breathing. It has an immediate connection to your emotional state. You breathe differently when you are tired, stressed, pessimistic or when you are excited, happy and peaceful. When practicing controlled breathing, you will immediately calm down and center your entire being. During the Mudra practice, the inhalation and exhalation should always be practiced thru the nose and remain centered at the solar plexus region. Place both palms of your hands on your stomach area and feel it expand with each inhalation and contract with each exhalation. Mudras are most often practiced in a slow, long and deep breathing rhythm.

Occasionally when so noted, you may use the fast, short breath of fire, which works under the same principles, but at a faster pace. With the breath of fire, the focus is on a more forceful exhalation, generated with a strong contracting movement of your stomach muscle. Always use your own judgment in regard to your breathing tempo, and remain comfortable during your Mudra practice. If needed, return back to the long, deep breathing to complete the recommended three-minute Mudra exercise. Remember, your breath holds the delicate balance between your physical body and your Soul. It keeps you alive, connected and present in this world and impacts every second of your life.

Posture & Eyes

The proper posture during Mudra practice is essential. A comfortable position with a straight back will allow all your subtle energy centers – Chakras and Nadis, to open up and function at their best capacity. Your shoulders should be in a fixed position and must not move during your breathing. The only motion is the expanding and contracting of your rib cage, accompanying each breath. During the Mudra practice, it is best to close your eyes, and gently direct the gaze towards the Third eye center. You can also keep them half open and lightly look over the tip of your nose. You may look into the middle-far away distance and relax the eyelids. Never force your fingers, hands, body or your eyes into a painful or uncomfortable position.

Meditation

During and after your Mudra practice, you will find yourself in a state of deep meditation. It will fell natural to remain still and enjoy the elevated state of consciousness. It is most beneficial to take advantage of this highly receptive and potent self-healing state. Continue with your long, deep breathing and allow your mind to settle into a most peaceful and serene demeanor of complete stillness. There are many types of meditation and you can use Mudras in combination with various meditation techniques. I suggest you do not preoccupy yourself with what you are supposed to experience, but simply allow the natural process to override any restless inner dialogue. Meditation is essential for cultivating your daily inner-calm and will greatly help you overcome various challenging situations. Approaching life with tranquility and a deep connection with the Divine will assist you in leading a happier and healthier life.

CONCENTRATION

Firmly hold your mind on a specific desired topic and direct your closed eyes towards your Third Eye area. Gently look slightly upward and direct your gaze far into the distance. That is your focus point where you can penetrate through the limited perception and glimpse into the higher realm of infinity. If you need an answer to a specific question, inquire your Higher consciousness. Only a clear question can receive a clear answer. Do not overanalyze. If you receive no answer, let go, and know that in due time your question will be answered.

VISUALIZATION

Your mind is an extremely powerful instrument. With the practice of Mudras and meditation you will learn to bring your mind into a state of absolute stillness and focus. You can practice visualization to help envision a healthy state of your body, a serendipitous circumstance, or a favorable outcome of an event. By visualizing a calming and healing environment, you can transform your well-being, reduce stress, and improve your overall health.

Visualization is equally important when you desire to attract love and abundance. Seeing yourself successful in your mind will attract circumstances and people who will help you succeed. Visualization is very easy and can be practiced anywhere. Mudra practice is an excellent opportunity to visualize the desired outcome. For example, when practicing the Mudra for Protecting your Health, visualize your body surrounded by vibrant restorative energy, filling you with brightest healing light. Create a powerful optimistic sphere where you can manifest your aspirations.

AFFIRMATIONS

During the Mudra practice your mind becomes receptive and open to positive input. This is an excellent time to consciously establish a positive inner dialogue, and use an affirmation of your choice. You may say the affirmation out loud before or after the Mudra practice, or repeat it in your mind during the entire exercise. Affirmations are always practiced with an openness that allows the Universe to bring about your wish, while you make an honest effort to help this become a reality. However, once you have done your part, allow the Universe to manifest the fulfillment of your desire in whatever way is best for you, and the higher good for all. Choose affirmations in a most positive sense and avoid using any negative words.

Affirm a positive outcome, a happy joyful state, optimal health and general optimism about your life. Repeat every word with true conviction, reflect on the meaning of it, while consciously embedding it into your mindset so that it becomes part of your healthy belief system and thinking pattern. A most powerful affirmation is your expression of gratitude. It carries wide reaching positive effects on all of your life circumstances. No matter how dire your situation, if you insist on finding elements you are grateful for, your effort will quickly overpower negative thought patterns in your mind. Your gratitude will attract positive and new energy into all areas of your life.

HOW LONG SHOULD YOU PRACTICE?

Each Mudra needs to be practiced at least three minutes. Allow two additional minutes for sitting in stillness and meditation. As little as this may seem, do not underestimate the power of Mudras. When you develop a regular practice you will feel the positive effects faster and stronger. A longer practice option is eleven minutes for each Mudra. You may practice as many Mudras as you wish. A combined thirty-minute daily Mudra and following meditation practice is an excellent and most beneficial routine. Ideal practice time is in the morning or late evening, before going to sleep.

MUDRAS AND MANTRAS

Mantras add a deeply transformative power of healing sound vibrations to your Mudra practice. Mantras resonate within your body in a most potent way. The hard palate in your mouth has fifty-eight power points that connect to your subtle body's energy meridians and affect your entire being. By singing, speaking, or whispering mantras, you are activating these energy points in a specific order and pattern that has a harmonious and healing effect on your physical, mental, emotional and spiritual body. The sound frequency resonates with each chakra and each cell of your body. The ancient science of mantras thus helps you reactivate and properly realign your chakras and nadis. In addition, mantras magnify your concentration, and are profoundly effective for stilling your mind. For example, when singing OM, you are affecting your entire body beginning at the First and ending at the Seventh Chakra. For a clear demonstration of the harmonious effect of sound on your body, take a long, deep breath and slowly sing A-E-I-O-U-M.

Feel the sound as it travels from your lower spine and ends with powerful vibration of MMM in your forehead. The healing frequency of this sound realigns your entire body.

Combining mantra and Mudra practice facilitates an experience of multidimensional healing. This technique activates your extra sensory abilities to help you recognize and work with the finest subtle frequencies that we obviously can't easily see or hear. As you sing mantras that apply to each Mudra, consciously perceive the frequency of your own voice, traveling from your throat towards the hands and back. Feel the harmonious resonance escalate and charge you with vital life force.

YOUR HANDS AND THE COSMOS

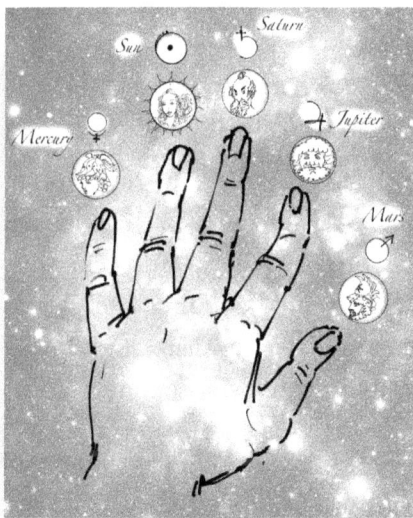

In addition to revitalizing your entire energy body, Mudras offer impressive benefits to accelerate your mental abilities, balance your emotions and elevate your state of consciousness. This specific effects occur when selected fingers are joined or kept apart, hands and palms turned in various directions, and each Mudra placed correctly in relation to your body. As I mentioned previously, Mudras are not isolated gestures, disconnected from your body's physical posture. All details such as the height and direction of the pointed fingers and palms are of the greatest importance, especially when your aim is to eliminate a challenging mental obstacle or increase a desired ability, improve a weakened state or develop and activate special gifts.

Our physical body also experiences a fascinating impact of the solar system. As mentioned on page 20 in Aura section, the right side of the body is ruled by the Sun, the male and mental aspect, and the left side is under the influence of the Moon, expressing your feminine, emotional energy. Furthermore, each finger relates to a specific planet, creating intricate network of interconnected triggers in your disposition, strengths, weaknesses, challenges as well as special abilities and gifts. This is one of the reasons why it is of significant importance which fingers connect and which hand is on top of the other, as well as where they are held in relation to your body.

Planetary Influence on Your Fingers

Thumb ~ MARS   God, willpower, logic, ego
Index ~ JUPITER   Knowledge, wisdom, self-confidence
Middle finger ~ SATURN   Patience, emotional control
Ring finger ~ SUN   Love, health, vitality, life energy
Little finger~ MERCURY   Communication, creativity, beauty

Benefits of Your Mudra Practice

Emotional and mental states continuously transform and shape your energy body in response to environment, other people and events that occur in your life. You may have a mentally, emotionally or spiritually challenging day, which won't necessarily show in your physical appearance, however your subtle energy body will absorb the disruptive energy and you will feel the consequences. Likewise, you could be going through an emotionally stressful situation, which won't visibly affect your physical body, but will definitely affect your energy body.

If these dynamics continue, your physical body will eventually display dis-ease as a result of long-term stressors on finer energy levels. You won't be able to ignore your issues and keep up the facade forever. If your everyday challenges are considerable, your subtle energy body will need to compromise as well as substitute for your energy depletion. Proper practice of Mudras will help release negative energy, limit the onset of disease and promote a healthy overall functioning. The beneficial effects will magnify with regular practice.

Mudras work on the finer, subtler energy levels that are invisible to the human eye. As a result, the benefits of Mudra practice are multi layered and reach far beyond simple physical improvements.

During Mudra practice, you are connecting the energy currents from two opposite poles of the right and left side of your body. This creates an energy surge, opens up blocked nadis and increases vital energy flow for regeneration and vitality.

In complex cases with long-term challenging emotional, physical or mental issues, we need to apply Mudra Therapy™ principles, which I describe in my book **MUDRA THERAPY**, *Hand Yoga for Pain Management and Conquering Illness.*

At the core of any self-improvement or self-help healing modality is the need for proper evaluation about the source and deeper nature of your challenge. Simply using the *Mudra for help with Stress* will help temporarily, but will be less effective for a long term solution, unless we eliminate the source of stress and disengage in stressful situations or dynamics. Finding and eliminating the source of stress is the crucial and deciding factor.

Similarly, *Mudra for a Healthy Diet* won't do you any good, if you continue to indulge in unhealthy eating patterns. In short, there is no escaping the need to find and address the core issue of your challenge. Once that is established, you can apply Mudras that will help you overcome, reprogram and discontinue unhealthy behavior and replace it with new and healthy habits.

Finally, when specifically using Mudras for help with PTSD, it is essential that you recognize and identify PTSD triggers and consciously release any negative patterns that may have been established recently or in your far-away past.

In the final healing step of this process, you will be able to recode your functioning habits and eliminate PTSD states that are detrimental to your overall health. This will create a healthy and resilient functioning template for your optimal physical, mental, emotional and spiritual wellbeing.

MUDRAS ARE YOUR ANCIENT KEYS TO UNLOCK
THE MAGNIFICENT POWER WITHIN.
ALL THE ANSWERS YOU ARE SEEKING ARE IN YOUR OWN HANDS.

Week One

II. IDENTIFY YOUR PTSD

While on this fascinating healing journey, we will be examining trauma from an esoteric perspective. This will offer you a much deeper and different view as well as potential for truly releasing and overcoming unharmonious and challenging consequences of a traumatic event or experience. It is in your subtle energy – etheric body where the clues reside, this is where you'll find the key to unraveling and healing your traumatic subtle energy imprint. It is invisible, yet overwhelmingly powerful.

If you address trauma just on the surface, you cannot expect a deep and thoroughly effective healing. You need to get to the core, into the realms of fine-subtle energy. This is what we shall be doing on our eight-week journey, step-by-step with patience, and attention to detail.

So we begin with the healing process by looking deeply, examining carefully, and taking into consideration various facts that may otherwise remain overlooked or ignored. The first thing you need to know about anything that you don't like or don't wish to have in your life, is a deeper understanding of what is the source of this uncomfortable aversion, dislike or fear. Most often we simply don't know and don't even want to look within. An invisible weight seems to linger on our shoulders, an unknown distaste, an allergy, a source of anxiety and inexplicable resistance, and we usually just accept it, as a normal part of life, our "nature," and choose to just live with it.

Why not take the time to look deeper and explore?
Why not look straight at the big elephant in the room and see what's it all about?
This is one of the most challenging tests of your willpower and character. It's time to tap into your reservoir of Soul power. It is no secret that precisely the least pleasant thing, topic

or person that we avoid, is actually the one we must eventually face. We don't have much choice with that.

Why? Because the mysterious reason that causes us to run in the opposite direction is perhaps a bigger challenge than we realize. In fact, it can be something that we brought with us from a long, long while back. Possibly even from another life.

CERTAIN PATTERNS THAT WE FIND OURSELVES IN ARE NOT A "NEW STORY." TRAUMA CAN SURVIVE LIFE AND DEATH.

This is truly an important fact to observe. Actually, we are often dealing with an old, even ancient story. It is your key to begin understanding why some difficulties are so deeply engrained into your psyche, that you can't seem to differentiate between what's normal or not. The thing is this: anything we are experiencing, no matter how challenging it is, seems normal to each one of us, especially if it reminds us of something from our recent of far past. We are sort of used to function in dysfunction. Just think about this:

ANYTHING AND EVERYTHING THAT HAPPENED TO US, HAS REMAINED IN OUR CELLULAR MATRIX SOUL - MEMORY.

This information is deep-set and helps us navigate through not one, but many lives. This is your invisible dictionary – the norm setter, the evaluator, the control dashboard.

Of course when we can't seem to find a clear and obvious reason that would explain a deep-set inclination, fear, resistance or aversion, it is wise to assume that we brought this challenge with us from long ago. Your Soul has carried this burden before. Obviously this leads to the conclusion that our deep-set trauma is not a new story, this is more like a repeat performance. Another opportunity for us to overcome, shift and outgrow.

Can we do it this time? Perhaps.
Is this easy to do? No.
This is one of your life's major challenges.
Is it possible to conquer? Absolutely.

In fact, old trauma that is deeply engrained in your soul psyche, and seems to navigate you throughout your life, reveals a certain part of your life purpose, mission or homework. But the big question remains: how much old trauma luggage are you carrying?

Just think about it. If for three lifetimes in a row, you experienced hardship with poverty and hunger, don't you think this will carry over into your current life and leave a deep seated fear of experiencing the same kind of challenge, yet again? You will simply assume that your next life will be the same. And even if you're born into entirely opposite set of circumstances, with a silver spoon in your mouth, you will still carry this fear, that shall follow you no matter what happens. It's in your cellular energy matrix.

An interesting example of that would be, when very often a famous or wealthy person lives in constant fear of losing money, lack of money, security, and feels in danger of being robbed of everything they have. Which of course in their case is quite ridiculous, because the opposite is true. But this old fear, an ancient trauma, prevents them from enjoying what they have now. So they are constantly sitting in a state of paranoid desperation and anxiety that their good fortune is only temporary. Their Post Traumatic Stress Disorder – PTSD, has extended into this life. It has survived their death and birth and is still lingering in their soul – etheric body. This kind of dynamic is what we are going to decipher, explore and examine. What is your old trauma and how it affects your current life, and how it relates to your new trauma?

YOUR ENERGY ANATOMY AND TRAUMA

First, let's look at the far away past and how the leftovers have possibly carried over into this lifetime. We'll find the connection of old – past life trauma, and the effect it has on your life now. This will prove to be a most fascinating and revealing discovery. When we look at the seven major chakras and what they are associated with, and pair them properly with the traumatized area of our life, we will clearly find the main seat of our fear, pain and congested subtle energy area.

> ANY AND ALL TRAUMATIC EVENTS LEAVE AN INVISIBLE,
> FINE ENERGY IMPRINT. LIKEWISE, PLEASANT MEMORIES
> ALSO REMAIN FOREVER IMPRINTED.

This explains unusual fondness and love for some things, places, and persons. The pleasant memories are connected with emotions of love. The unpleasant ones are connected with emotions of fear. When we are in love, our individual frequency vibrates at the highest level possible – for your individual capacity.

All expressions of love uplift and elevate your frequency. On the other side of the spectrum, where negativity rules and fear is king, the individual frequency drops into the lower realms. Therefore this negative information creates a denser energy field. This "sphere or cluster" of negative lower frequency, remains in your system unless you consciously overcome it, or manage to release it. If it remains in your system and magnifies in size, it eventually creates a serious problem that affects all of your subtle energy body layers, your mental and emotional body, and finally also your physical body.

YOUR PAST LIFE CHAKRA – TRAUMA REVIEW

FIRST CHAKRA

Let's say you are challenged in the area of the first chakra. The trauma that is connected to this center has to do with the fight for survival, feeling confident that you belong in this world, and are able to maintain a healthy, strong sense of positively sustainable energy flow. If your far – away past entailed an extreme case of poverty, starvation, lack of survival skills, then this old memory will sit deeply in the first energy center, maintaining an energy block that is problematic for you, even in this life. You will feel stuck in survival mode, even if there is no reason for such existential fear in the present life.

SECOND CHAKRA

If your challenges are in the area of creative expression, sexuality, and the physical aspects of interacting within relationships and partnerships, your challenge has to do with a traumatic experience in the second chakra. It could be anything from past physical abuse, physical dysfunctions connected with rape, or unpleasant physical contact experiences. In case of creativity, it would indicate that your creative gift was unsupported, not accepted, perhaps even ridiculed or punished. This old resistance will keep an invisible field of impenetrable hesitation, that will prevent you from experiencing deep and rewarding physical closeness. In respect to your creative expression, you might be fighting with self-imposed hesitation, self-doubt, and fear-induced inability to express your creativity.

THIRD CHAKRA

In third chakra your trauma is connected with the mind and your ego. If your ego was destroyed in the far away past, or challenges were created because of your overactive mind, or perhaps your intellect was under-appreciated, ridiculed, punished, ignored, as a consequence this would leave an imprint of feeling fearful to reveal your mind power. Perhaps you missed an important observation, or made a mistake in intellectual assessment, wrong decision, which may claimed your own, or another person's life. This trauma will remain in your third chakra area of your subtle energy field. It will leave you with a severe case of low self-esteem, lack of courage, self-doubt, and weakened or fearful expression of your mind power. This is connected with fear of failure, or dread of repeating the traumatic event.

FOURTH CHAKRA

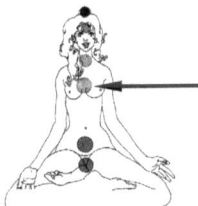

If your past trauma occurred in the matters of the heart, love, receiving and giving love, perhaps with an exceptionally traumatic heartbreak, separation, loss of loved one, betrayal, unrequited love, grief, or rejected love, this will leave a traumatic pattern that will sit in your heart and in this lifetime you will – for seemingly unknown reasons – feel unloved, undesirable, unwanted, undeserving, mistrusting, fearful of betrayal, abandonment and unworthy of love.

FIFTH CHAKRA

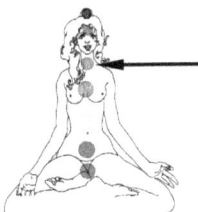

If your past trauma has to do with speaking your truth – the essence of your fifth chakra, perhaps you were previously punished for revealing the truth, speaking your mind, and your only way to survive was to remain silent, say things you didn't mean, or even lie. This survival pattern will remain in your energy matrix. As a result – in your present life – you may be fearful of speaking the truth and feel compelled to lie, even if you are completely unthreatened. This way you will simply create unnecessary problems for yourself by telling falsehoods, when speaking the truth would serve you much better. If this was a survival skill of your past, it is understandable. If you were punished for speaking up, you will struggle with the ability to vocally and verbally represent and express yourself in this lifetime.

SIXTH CHAKRA

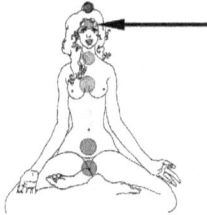

If your past trauma is connected to the sixth chakra, it relates to the sense of intuition. If in the far away past your intuition failed you, which caused you to misinterpret a certain situation or a person, and you suffered consequences of great loss, or even death, you will have a dense and congested energy field in the area of the sixth chakra. It will prevent you from trusting your own intuition this time around, and you will constantly struggle with following your sixth sense. Self-doubt, extreme and obsessive mind dwelling, and logical overthinking will be your challenging impulse. You will fear making a similar error as you did in your far away past, and will find yourself very resistant to believing, trusting, or even recognizing your own sense of intuition.

SEVENTH CHAKRA

If the trauma is connected to the seventh chakra, it would indicate that in the far away past, you experienced a seeming disappointment in your sense and understanding of Universal power, God and faith. Perhaps you were abused in the house of worship or by someone in a position of authority representing a religion. Maybe you passively relied on and hoped for Divine intervention, which remained elusive. It is possible your survival was hanging in balance and you remained too passive, and as a repercussion the misfortune was momentous, through loss of your dear ones or your own life. This created a deep-seated fear that you were betrayed, forgotten, abandoned or even ignored by the Divine power or God. This kind of trauma experience will create a general lack of faith, negativity, pessimism, bitterness, victimhood and an overall fearful, passive disposition. Your fear will be expressed through deep aversion to anything associated with religion, and people in power of representing it. You will carry a wounded sense of abandonment and deep-seated melancholy.

THE HIDDEN TRAUMA

The old past-life trauma is most often completely forgotten. This is understandable since we begin this new life with a clean slate. To work through these deeply seated fears and remains of old trauma, one is required to do introspective inner work, and tediously look for connective elements and details. You can and will find them. The good news is, that the trauma is less raw in this present life, and you can recognize and observe this process with a conscious step-by-step approach, and gain a deeper understanding of your inner makings. Recognizing the magnitude, extent and influence of your far-past on your current disposition will be very revealing, productive and positive. In addition, you will gain a sense of broader understanding about the limitations of time, the reincarnation process, the karmic principles, and most importantly, the main mission of your current life. Old past-life trauma does not remain hidden or forgotten by coincidence. It is part of the incarnation process that we forget all our past and start fresh.

**A DEEP SEATED PAST-LIFE MEMORY
REMAINS IN THE SUBTLE ENERGY CELLULAR SENSORY MATRIX,
BUT THE WOUNDS ARE ONLY PARTIALLY HEALED,
AND NOT COMPLETELY FORGOTTEN.**

If we could remember all our challenges from our past lives, it would be simply too much to bear. We would fear the horror, pain, trauma and loss we have endured in the past, and this would make it impossibly challenging for us to "give it another go."

The trauma that is hidden under the veils of incarnation is very different, than the hidden trauma from this – current lifetime. The concealed trauma from current lifetime has to do with denial. It is a survival reflex that helps us move along and pretend that something never happened. We may do this consciously or unconsciously. We know and are somewhat aware that trauma happened, but we are not dealing with it, not resolving it or balancing out the damaging or challenging effects that were left behind. We simply pretend it never happened.

**THE PROBLEM WITH IGNORING CURRENT-LIFE TRAUMA
IS THAT SOMEDAY, WHEN WE LEAST EXPECT IT
AND WHEN IT IS MOST INCONVENIENT,
THIS OLD TRAUMA WILL RESURFACE AND FORCE US TO FACE IT.**

THE FORGOTTEN TRAUMA

Forgetting a past-life trauma is different. It is our subconscious that has blocked out a traumatic event and we simply have no easily accessible memory of it. However, this forgetfulness is only temporary and superficial. In our current mindset we may have temporarily forgotten it, but in our deeper soul-memory, we carry the information within our ethereal matrix.

PAST LIFE PTSD INFORMATION STILL AFFECTS YOUR CURRENT LIFE DECISIONS AND CHOICES.

Forgotten trauma remains deeply ingrained, almost as a kind of survival instinct, that helps us focus on positive potential in our new life. It is like a new program, installed for the purpose of helping you avoid damaging consequences of past traumatic experiences, while selectively remembering only the constructive part of the past experience.

For example, if in a past life a person died from a drug overdose, chances are in this life they will have a severe aversion to any kind of drugs. But of course this can be considerably more complex, as there are countless possibilities. If they have not learned their lesson, they may succumb to drugs again in this lifetime.

ADDICTION CARRIES OVER, AS DO ALL EXTREME ATTACHMENTS THAT WE HAVE EXPERIENCED IN EARTHLY REALM.

The imprint remains, it is up to us, how we will use that information – in a positive or negative way. If the past-life trauma is connected to a specific person that is again present in our current life and that we have to interact with, we will experience a subconscious reincarnation-amnesia or memory loss. This gives us an opportunity to work on that specific relationship with renewed optimism and hope. But that does not mean that we are out of the woods yet. The traumatic patterns that involve others are often repeated through many lifetimes, while we're always encountering either the same problem or usually with the same person. The karmic aspect of this process is very complex and difficult to thoroughly understand. However, suffice it to say, the purpose always remains similar: to find a harmonious resolve, grow from the experience and neutralize any animosity that is carried over.

NEGATIVE MEMORIES AND EXPERIENCES KEEP US CAPTIVE IN THE WHEEL OF REINCARNATION.

The more loving and higher our natural frequency becomes, the lighter our burden, and the better our chances of ascension. In simple terms: unresolved trauma keeps us coming back to this Earthly realm, in order to overcome, harmonize and eliminate the lower-bound frequency that keeps us captive in this dimension.

It's a tricky circle, to say the least. So you see, simply forgetting an old trauma does have a price. We cannot move forward in a healthy, fully empowered way, until we understand all our complex aspects and our innermost psychological makings and tendencies. Once that is accomplished, our ascension process is possible and assured.

When old trauma remains unresolved and affects every singular action, behavior, expectation and choice in your life, this requires deep inner work and much patience to recognize, analyze, discover, and uncover old events that can immediately shed light onto all complex dynamics of your current life challenges.

On final note, it is wise and constructive to see and embrace the following:

**TRAUMA IS A CHALLENGING EXPERIENCE
THAT CARRIES IMMENSE POTENTIAL FOR GROWTH,
WISDOM AND ACCELERATED PROGRESS
ON YOUR SPIRITUAL ASCENSION JOURNEY.**

Yes, this Earthly plane is beautiful, but it is also quite intensely dark, with a powerful downward force, pulling us in all possible hazardous directions.

We are here for a reason, we each have a purpose. Figuring it out is the key. And believe it or not, most often trauma carries the secret ingredient that helps our soul in indescribable ways. Our life here is to be enjoyed, but we must also learn and eventually graduate beyond. Some aspects are very deceptive. Material wealth has nothing to do with spiritual wealth. You can't buy true love and you can't buy a lifetime worth of wisdom. Those things you have to earn through experience.

**THE VALUE SYSTEMS OF EARTH AND SPIRIT WORLD
ARE TWO POLAR OPPOSITES.
IN THAT CASE, TRAUMA IS A BLESSING IN DISGUISE.**

FINDING THE SOURCE

I f you are ready to look at your past trauma in order to prepare for a conscious release and healing, the easiest approach is to explore and find the areas in your chakra system that contain energy blockages.

How can you do that? Any type of physical challenge that you are suffering from have to do with the specific chakra, as mentioned previously. Finding the source is very important part of your healing journey. It is truly essential. Hiding the source of old and past trauma is a bad idea.

Why? Some people may think that the less they talk about it, the less effect the trauma will keep having, but unfortunately this is not so. It is a bit more complicated than just sweeping old pain under the rug and pretending everything is fine. The more you hide the pain, the heavier it will become. Just think about it; you are carrying extra weight and no one knows about it. This demands an extra energy effort that you are required to put into any activity, interaction or relationship in order to maintain the false image of an entirely different person than you really are. Trauma often leaves feelings of humiliation and shame and in order to ignore these feelings, much counter projected energy is required.

Eventually the unbearable energy strain will become a subtle-energy blockage cluster, and create a physical manifestation of all that negative energy.

THE SUBTLE ENERGY BODY'S TOXIC OR NEGATIVE OVERLOAD WILL EVENTUALLY EXPAND BEYOND THE INVISIBLE ENERGY FIELD AND MATERIALIZE IN YOUR PHYSICAL BODY AS DISEASE.

A visible consequence will appear as the final physical manifestation of the energy imbalance – an illness. Now, we are forced to acknowledge there is a problem, because we can't pretend it's not there. Your physical body is simply forcing you to deal with the issue. But all this is preventable, if you are aware and consciously research, explore and resolve your body's possible area of trauma congestion.

IDENTIFY THE NATURE OF YOUR PAST-LIFE PTSD

PTSD indicates remaining effects of a PAST trauma, be it from current or previous lifetime. Something occurred that had such a profound effect on your general experience of life, that it altered your belief system, your physical condition, mental state and emotional resilience. It shattered you to the core. But often we don't even know what it was. It's like a permanent shadow lurking in the depths of our being.

Now it's time to find it, confront it and abolish it. But before we do, remember to keep an eye out for finding the small grain of wisdom. This is invaluable and will stay in your treasure chest of knowledge. It is your reward, your payback, your karmic royalty payment, shall we say.

The clues may be in the smallest of details. Remember, nothing is perfect in any family dynamic and everything that happened to us up until and including this very moment is a supremely complex mixture of circumstances, great gifts, rewards, old debts, new journeys, explorations, fears and unfulfilled loves that we need to face or deservingly enjoy.

PERFECTION ON THIS EARTHLY REALM IS NONEXISTENT.

Perfection of ethereal realms is unattainable. So it seems that your best option is to decipher this very present moment – the here and now, and make the very best of it.

CHAKRA - TRAUMA SCALE
OF YOUR PAST OR CURRENT TRAUMA

Let's look at this scale to help you assess the deep source of distress – past-life old trauma that can't be traced to any event in this life, or trauma location that is clearly associated with an event that occurred in this lifetime.

CHAKRA ONE

SURVIVAL – This causes you greatest distress and preoccupies your life.
QUESTION: Is your cause for concern justifiable or exaggerated?
ORIGIN in PAST LIFE: You can't find a reason why you fear for your survival.
CURRENT LIFE: Your trauma in this area is recent, you know the source or cause.

CHAKRA TWO

CREATIVITY – This unexpressed aspect is your source of discontent.
QUESTION: Is your reason for ignoring your creativity clear or unknown?
ORIGIN in PAST LIFE: You can't find a reason why you hesitate or abstain.
CURRENT LIFE: Your trauma in this area is recent, you know the source or cause.

CHAKRA THREE

MIND ~EGO – These aspects are greatly challenged.
QUESTION: Are you exaggerating your self-criticism or sense of importance?
ORIGIN in PAST LIFE: You can't see why you doubt your intellect or value.
CURRENT LIFE: Your trauma in this area is recent, you know the source or cause.

CHAKRA FOUR

LOVE – This is your main source of heartache and sorrow.
QUESTION: Is your disposition closed-off or overextended in sacrifice?
ORIGIN in PAST LIFE: You can't see why you are a recluse and closed off.
CURRENT LIFE: Your trauma in this area is recent, you know the source or cause.

CHAKRA FIVE

COMMUNICATION – This is your greatest weakness – inability, or constant speaking.
QUESTION: Are you silent or overly talkative on purpose or in fear?
ORIGIN in PAST LIFE: You can't control your timid or incessant disposition.
CURRENT LIFE: Your trauma in this area is recent, you know the source or cause.

CHAKRA SIX

INTUITION – You are incapable of recognizing or following your intuition.
QUESTION: Are you avoiding responsibility for finding answers, making choices?
ORIGIN in PAST LIFE: You are afraid or incapable of trust when going within.
CURRENT LIFE: Your trauma in this area is recent, you know the source or cause.

CHAKRA SEVEN

DIVINE UNITY – You are disconnected from God or having faith.
QUESTION: Are you afraid of truth, death or punishment?
ORIGIN in PAST LIFE: You have a fear or aversion to religion in general sense.
CURRENT LIFE: Your trauma in this area is recent, you know the source or cause.

CHAKRA TRAUMA SCALE

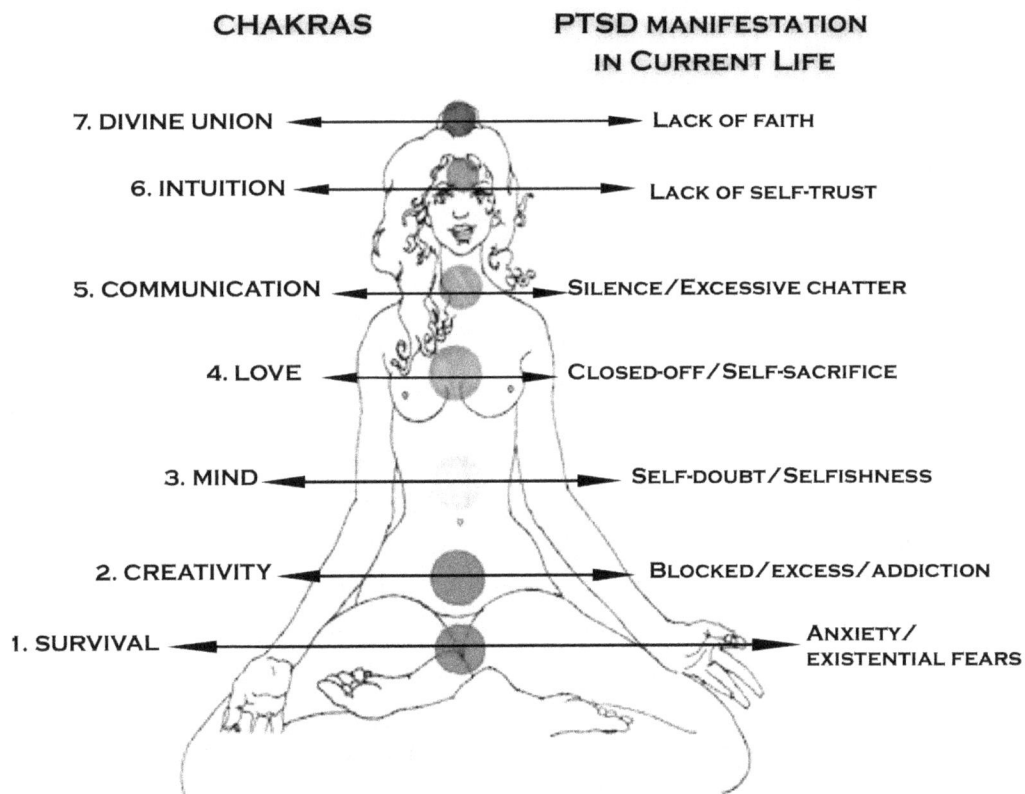

CHAKRAS	PTSD MANIFESTATION IN CURRENT LIFE
7. DIVINE UNION	LACK OF FAITH
6. INTUITION	LACK OF SELF-TRUST
5. COMMUNICATION	SILENCE/EXCESSIVE CHATTER
4. LOVE	CLOSED-OFF/SELF-SACRIFICE
3. MIND	SELF-DOUBT/SELFISHNESS
2. CREATIVITY	BLOCKED/EXCESS/ADDICTION
1. SURVIVAL	ANXIETY/EXISTENTIAL FEARS

YOUR ASSIGNMENT

AFFIRMATION

UNCOVERING MY DEEPEST SECRETS WILL REVEAL MY GREATEST GIFTS

DIARY

This week you are working thru self-assessment to clarify (for your-eyes-only) the following:
- Identifying the connection between your past-life trauma and current experiences.
- Finding the area of your energy congestion on chakra-trauma scale.

What was your childhood support system?

How did your parents play a supportive or a challenging role?

What were your adolescence challenges?

What is your current main trauma challenge?

How are you experiencing this today?

Your goal for resolving trauma?

PROCESS

Work thru the questions, come back in a few days, see if anything changed, add it on, clarify, clean it up, and self-discover through the process.

PRACTICE

This first week is journaling time for you. Make a conscious effort to remember your childhood circumstances in a most objective way. Write it all down and read as if you were reviewing notes from someone else. Create a self-imposed space between your past and your present, between your trauma and yourself. Reflect and clarify your current goal. Sleep on it. Continue the next day. Next week, we will add Mudra practice to your healing regimen. Smile…every day.

**YOU ARE ON A SELF - EXPLORATORY JOURNEY.
YOUR MISSION IS TO HEAL
ON THE DEEPEST LEVEL OF YOUR SOUL.**

TRAUMA IN YOUR CHILDHOOD

1. WHAT SUPPORT IF ANY, DID YOU RECEIVE FROM YOUR MOTHER?

2. WHAT WORD BEST DESCRIBES YOUR RELATIONSHIP WITH YOUR MOTHER?

3. WHAT SUPPORT IF ANY, DID YOU RECEIVE FROM YOUR FATHER?

4. WHAT WORD BEST DESCRIBES YOUR RELATIONSHIP WITH YOUR FATHER?

5. WHAT SUPPORT IF ANY, DID YOU RECEIVE FROM YOUR SIBLINGS, COUSINS OR FRIENDS?

6. WHAT SUPPORT IF ANY, DID YOU RECEIVE FROM YOUR TEACHERS OR GRANDPARENTS?

7. WHAT WAS YOUR BIGGEST CHALLENGE OR CHILDHOOD TRAUMA?

8. WHAT HAVE YOU DONE TO HEAL THIS WOUND?

TRAUMA IN YOUR ADOLESCENCE

1. WHAT SUPPORT IF ANY, DID YOU RECEIVE FROM YOUR MOTHER?

2. HOW DID YOUR RELATIONSHIP WITH YOUR MOTHER CHANGE DURING THIS TIME?

3. WHAT SUPPORT IF ANY, DID YOU RECEIVE FROM YOUR FATHER?

4. HOW DID YOUR RELATIONSHIP WITH YOUR FATHER CHANGE DURING THIS TIME?

5. WHO WAS YOUR CLOSEST ALLY?

6. WHAT BROUGHT YOU MOST JOY?

7. WHAT WAS YOUR BIGGEST CHALLENGE OR TRAUMA?

8. WHAT WAS YOUR DREAM FOR YOUR FUTURE?

TRAUMA IN YOUR ADULTHOOD

1. WHAT HAS BEEN YOUR MOST TRAUMATIC EVENT?

2. HOW HAS THIS AFFECTED YOU?

3. DO YOU FEEL YOU'VE HEALED YOUR WOUNDS?

4. DO YOU STILL SUFFER FROM CONSEQUENCES?

5. HAS YOUR TRAUMA FOLLOWED YOU TO THIS DAY?

6. WHAT IS YOUR MOST VULNERABLE AND FEARFUL BELIEF?

7. IS THIS CONNECTED TO OLD OR NEW TRAUMA?

8. WHAT IS YOUR BIGGEST STRENGTH, ABILITY AND GIFT?

9. IS THIS A POSITIVE RESULT OF OLD OR NEW TRAUMA?

10. WHAT IS YOUR CURRENT BIGGEST CHALLENGE?

11. IS IT CONNECTED TO YOUR PAST OR NEW TRAUMA?

12. WHAT ASPECT OF YOURSELF AND YOUR LIFE DO YOU WISH TO HEAL, RESOLVE, IMPROVE AND EMPOWER?

EXAMINE THE WOUND

YOUR ANCIENT BRUISE

Now that you have a clearer insight into the source and origins of your past traumatic experience, you can embark on the next step of your healing process: examining the depth, subtle energy congested area, and consistency of your wound.

Last week you reflected on the possible connections of your trauma with your unknown far-away past life. To put it simply – if you can't find the cause of your deep-set trauma in this lifetime, it most likely stems from an old pattern and an ancient old wound.

In your questionnaire, you also reviewed the possible occurrence of trauma in this lifetime. It may not have been entirely pleasant, but it needed to be done. Everything you have the courage to face, becomes instantly smaller once the looming darkness of fear dissipates.

This process has also helped you narrow down and eliminate the feeling of confusion. Old traumatic experiences that are buried in your depth, linger there while persistently emitting unpleasant, disruptive subtle energy. You may generally feel incredibly discontent, fearful, but for no apparent reason.

CHILDHOOD TRAUMA IS OFTEN FORGOTTEN OR BLOCKED OUT.

By examining all possible sources, you are getting closer, narrowing it down and regaining control of who you are, and who you can and will be, as it relates to your life's future opportunities and upcoming relationships. With each step you are closer to reclaiming your inner peace, sense of order and clarity.

In this next phase of the healing process, you will learn fascinating information about your subtle energy body and its role in your trauma release. If your trauma stems from this lifetime, you know the source and can approach the healing a bit differently. But let's begin with the older cause of trauma, stemming from your far away past. The positive side of the situation where a challenge traveled with your soul energy through many lifetimes, is that you can use this new awareness wisely. This is your opportunity to consciously release any negative feelings towards situations, people, circumstances in this current life, that are not caused by a current upset. How?

RECOGNIZE THAT YOUR EMOTIONAL OR MENTAL REPERCUSSIONS YOU MAY BE EXPERIENCING HERE AND NOW, HAVE NOTHING TO DO WITH PEOPLE OR SITUATIONS IN THIS LIFETIME.

They seem to unknowingly trigger your past trauma. It is a case of "mistaken identity." You simply assume someone or a situation is causing you pain, when in fact the pain is within you, not from the current outside situation. It is an old pain that has traveled with you to the present time and continues to unnecessarily traumatize you. For example, perhaps you carry a deep fear of betrayal and unfairly accuse everyone that is near you, that they are betraying you. They may not be betraying you at all, but you have a deeply engrained reason to assume and anticipate it.

If you look at the situation from this new perspective, you will leave the option open that this person here and now, has never betrayed you. Most likely they never will. Therefore your fear about betrayal makes no sense. This openness and triumph over your rigid presumption will help you overcome a negative mindset that is in your way.

Another example would be: if your past trauma left you with severe anxiety around detecting smoke in the air, and nothing distressing in connection with smoke has ever happened to you in this life, you can begin to understand that this distress and fear was caused by an old trauma, that has apparently carried over. This kind of examination of your general, inexplicable deep-set fears, will help understand a lot of other tendencies and most of all, you will begin understanding your own actions, decisions, choices and aversions. All these are connected to something old and nothing new from your current life. This allows you to realize in an unthreatening way, that in this lifetime, nothing challenging happened to you in these areas, and therefore you can begin healing and letting go of your self-induced stressed state. Yes, the fear may be deep-set, but your understanding will help you in letting go.

Why? Because the distress from previous lifetime obviously did not repeat itself in this lifetime. Which means that not everything ends up always in the same predicament as it did before. You can shift your perception, open up to the possibility that in this lifetime nothing of such identical trauma will happen. This is a much more common issue than you may imagine. It is very present in many people's lives.

WE ALL HAVE TO OVERCOME THE FEARS FROM OUR FAR-AWAY PAST.

This release will free up your energy body of unnecessary old trauma and help you dissolve the congested energy cluster. You will be able to open up to new and positive experiences. Another example would be that in a past life you experienced a very traumatic loss of a dear person. In this lifetime this may have carried over as a case of extreme paranoia, anxiety or fear that you will lose someone or anyone near and dear to you. In fact, this post traumatic state will have absolutely nothing to do with this lifetime, but every time you will find yourself emotionally close to another person, the old fear will begin rising up and affecting your current relationship. For seemingly unknown reasons you will dread the loss of dear one, without any tangible or logical explanation.

Judging yourself or being judged by others that you have an issue, a problem or a phobia, will strain your emotional state even more. But, if you search and can not find any such occurrence in this lifetime, you can recognize that this is indeed a very old trauma that simply carried over into your current lifetime. There is another very powerful aspect to this particular dynamic. The old fears and traumas may not always be present. They may inexplicably emerge just with one, very particular person.

For example, perhaps you never feared losing someone and went through relationships in the usual ways. But then unexpectedly, a particular person that you meet, triggers a subconscious fear-reflex, connected to a very frightening event from your deep memory. You feel shaken to the core in fear of losing them or any other possible scenario that is emotionally very distressing. This old trigger creates a tension in the current relationship without any particular clear reason. You simply find yourself responding in an unusual way specifically in this particular relationship dynamic – or exclusively in regards to this one person.

If you never felt this particular kind of fear before, this is a most certain indicator that your past life trauma occurred only with this particular person. This is of course challenging, but also quite fascinating and has a profound purpose. You have received an opportunity to heal the past together in this lifetime, by overcoming the pain of separation and finally relax into the opportunity for a happy manifestation of your relationship in current life.

Your unfulfilled and denied love of your past was so great, that it brought you together once again, so you can fulfill your desire to be together while healing your past. This time your purpose is to realize the power of love, but also gain the ability to understand, that the precise scenario from years ago will not repeat itself again. This is a wonderful opportunity to speak about it, be open, receptive, and slowly understand the source of your unfounded fear or PTSD, and eventually completely overcome it and truly heal your ancient wound.

YOUR RECENT WOUND

If your wound is recent, the approach is very different. You are not left in the dark as to when and what happened. You have been spared the discovery search. But you are facing a heavier load in the effort to harmonize something that is much more raw and vivid in your memory, because after all, it happened just a short while ago, even if the trauma happened in your childhood.

The point is that it happened in this lifetime and you are possibly still in similar geographical or physical environment where the trauma occurred. If others were involved, you most likely also know of your wrongdoers existence and whereabouts. Perhaps you have to face them every day. But there is a possibility that even if the trauma happened in this lifetime, you have forgotten or buried it in your subconscious mind, so you could survive the initial shock.

The healing process can and will occur in both cases, but certainly with certain adjustments. Another very common occurrence is, that the negative person who caused or is otherwise connected to your trauma in this lifetime, was with you in the far away past as well – in such a case this is the opportunity to heal, despite the fact that what connects you is an old negative experience.

This does not mean that you have or will achieve peace with that person, it means that they will not be able to harm you anymore and certainly not again. The realization and deep recognition of your unharmonious connection, will help you become more resilient and eventually immune to their negative effects.

YOU CAN'T FIGHT SOMETHING YOU CAN'T SEE OR RECOGNIZE.

Once you recognize the source, you can face it with empowered clarity and triumph over it. So whatever circumstance of past trauma that bonded you two together through past lifetimes, can be looked as another chance to heal, overcome, and neutralize the negative energy exchange.

> **YOU CAN HEAL AND DISSOLVE THE NEGATIVE ATTACHMENT THAT BINDS YOU TO ANOTHER PERSON.**

This brings us to the next important exploration for deeper understanding of the complex nature of energy anatomy. So you see, in order to heal the aftereffects of current or very recent trauma, you need to be aware of all possible scenarios, that bind you to a repeated challenging experiences. Recent trauma that happened in your childhood will leave very different subtle energy residual effect in your body, than distress experienced in your adulthood. Childhood trauma is lingering in the chakra area that is connected to the corresponding development stage and physical age.

YOUR CHILDHOOD TRAUMA CORRESPONDING TO CHAKRA SCALE

There are endless possibilities as to what kind of trauma occurred, but what matters here is the age factor. The years correspond to specific Chakras. This way you can find the main issue that is consistently challenging for you, as it relates to the time of occurrence in your childhood. This sets up a pattern for adulthood, where repercussions of childhood trauma remain and further shape your life.

TRAUMA AT AGE ONE – affects all aspects of CHAKRA 1 ~ SURVIVAL

Can manifest as: persistent existential fear, issues with feeling physically, materially safe

TRAUMA AT AGE TWO – affects all aspects of CHAKRA 2 ~ CREATIVITY, SEX

Can manifest as: creative suppression, sexual dysfunction, jealousy, envy

TRAUMA AT AGE THREE – affects all aspects of CHAKRA 3 ~ MIND, EGO

Can manifest as: over-analyzing, ego imbalance, insecurity, need for attention, narcissism

TRAUMA AT AGE FOUR – affects all aspects of CHAKRA 4 ~ LOVE

Can manifest as: unworthiness, difficulty receiving and giving, lack of affection, resisting love

TRAUMA AT AGE FIVE – affects all aspects of CHAKRA 5 ~ COMMUNICATION

Can manifest as: not speaking your truth, excessive talk, restless inner dialogue

TRAUMA AT AGE SIX – affects all aspects of CHAKRA 6 ~ INTUITION

Can manifest as: self-doubt, skeptical of your sixth sense, suspicious, co-dependent

TRAUMA AT AGE SEVEN – affects all aspects of CHAKRA 7 ~ UNIVERSAL LAW

Can manifest as: distrust, no faith, atheism, hopelessness, disbelief, fear of abandonment

YOUR NATURAL SURVIVAL INSTINCT

This is something very individual and unique. We each have certain deep-set reflexes, extra abilities and self-preservation skills. Most of them are similar to others, but there are some that have to do with what you have learned as a soul, throughout your many lives. And this can certainly never be identical to someone else. Similar – yes, but identical – no. It is akin to exceptional unique gifts and talents that you have. Your old memory is not selective in remembering only things you were good at. It also remembers things you learned that were dangerous, unhealthy or good and healing. This hard-earned knowledge and wisdom always plays an important role in your choices and decisions, especially if they need to happen unexpectedly, in the spur of the moment.

YOUR ADAPTED SURVIVAL SKILLS

These skills have to do with you adjusting your reaction and disposition towards various elements and events in a way that is highly reactive, defensive, protective, overly suspicious, exaggerated or frightened. Your survival reflex will take all these after-effects into consideration and apply all possible options to your assessment process. It will be harder for you to give people the benefit of the doubt, think optimistically, or be open to new unusual experiences that have nothing to do with your past, but may somehow remind you of it.

NEGATIVE MEMORIES LEAVE TRACES OF LIMITED BELIEFS, BASED ON FEARS AND TRAUMA. REMAIN OPEN-MINDED AND GAIN AN OPPORTUNITY TO OVERCOME RESTRICTED BELIEF SYSTEM.

YOUR AURA AND PTSD

We know that the physical body that we see with our human eyes, is only the coarse manifestation layer of who you truly are. In other words, you are much more than just your physical body. In fact, you energy body is quite larger in size and magnitude.

There are numerous fine layers of invisible subtle energy that envelop your physical body and hold unique information about your essence and frequency. The emotional layer contains information filled with your personal emotional expression.

For example: if your emotions are mostly in the form of fear, this will be lingering in your subtle emotional body. No matter what you do, where you go, how you train your physical body, or appear strong and mighty, deep inside you will still feel fearful, because your emotional layer carries that information frequency. This is most often observed in people who are mighty in size and appearance, but underneath that facade of a mountain of a person, lies a very frightened, shy, and insecure little person. It is almost as if the Universe granted a fearful person a mighty body, in order to help them overcome the past, filled with a sense of physical inferiority and fear of weakness. This kind of dynamic can be found in endless combinations.

For example; someone not particularly or traditionally beautiful, perhaps even a bit odd looking by the current norm (whatever that may be), may carry an aura of indescribable appeal and unusual beauty. You see, their emotional body is confident, glowing and assured that beauty comes from within the soul that carries ancient information.

IF A SOUL HAS A BEAUTIFUL, LOVING, HIGH FREQUENCY, IT WILL EMIT A POWERFUL AND MAGNETIC GLOW, NO MATTER WHAT THE PHYSICAL EXTERIOR LOOKS LIKE.

Same principles apply to other emotional states and conditions. You can have a negative, unpleasant person that seems to look beautiful by the current standards, but their overall frequency will exude an unpleasant, negative frequency no matter how they adorn their physical body. Their energy essence is simply unpleasant. And an energy sensitive person will be able to easily detect this.

However, a less energy perceptive person will be blinded by their seeming physical beauty. Likewise, a subtle energy receptive person will be able to detect the state of a fearful giant, or insecure person in position of power. No matter how much power they are given, in their essence, they still suffer from debilitating insecurities. One could say that all these traumatized states that have to do with our character are really quite complex.

Various PTSD dynamics are carried over from such a long time ago, that nobody can remember them. This entire view of complex situations will reveal an incredible field of possibilities for your deep, conscious, and transformative healing to occur. The process is an internal, restorative journey. Full participation is required in order to intentionally reposition the balance of inner power.

TEARS in AURIC SHIELD

When inflicted trauma is intense, the impact reverberates through all the subtle energy layers, and often inflicts an injury to your auric shield. This can manifest in a form of a tear, that creates a vulnerable opening for more long-term damage. An example would be when an auric tear happens from a heavy physical wound, or a person loses a limb, and they still feel the subtle energy presence of the injured limb, despite the fact that it is physically gone. What they are connecting their sensory experience with, is their subtle energy body. However, in the place of injury, their auric field has a tear, which creates a subtle energy "leak."

PHYSICAL INJURY IS NOT THE ONLY WAY TO INFLICT AN AURIC TEAR. MIND ALTERING SUBSTANCES POSE ANOTHER GREAT DANGER FOR AN AURIC TEAR IN THE FINE SUBTLE LAYER OF MENTAL ENERGY BODY.

If a person succumbs to prolonged drug use, their auric shield will weaken and become easily penetrable. Emotional abuse will not create a direct tear, however, an oversaturated subtle energy congestion from severe emotional pain, could reach such a level of density that it would weaken the auric shield and prevent it from functioning properly. If this dynamic is ongoing for long term, with time an auric shield tear will happen in the emotional subtle energy area, closely connected to the nature of trauma. Once a tear is created, the person becomes vulnerable to energy leaks, overall weakness as well as openness to attack from negative energy entities and forces.

If your auric shield tear is in the second chakra, connected to creativity and sexuality, you could fall victim to a similar trauma, just because you are depleted and weak in precisely that energy center. A negative exchange with someone else will have bigger damaging effects on you, as opposed to you remaining naturally resilient and almost untouchable.

Example: A person has been in a physically abusive relationship, and the trauma created an auric tear which will continue to present ongoing danger, even with another partner. They will almost certainly attract a similar dysfunctional dynamic, because their weakened energy state has a vulnerability that exposes them to preying, and abusive personalities.

Example: A person who damaged their auric shield with drugs, will need to fight to resist ongoing temptation to succumb to drugs, because their auric tear leaves them exposed and vulnerable to similar subtle energy frequency of energy draining, and destructive people who engage with these activities.

Example: A person who has endured or witnessed extremely violent experiences, perhaps through war, or some kind of physical assault. Their auric shield is wounded and completely vulnerable to negative vibrations in any form. As a result, that may easily and quickly overwhelm their entire persona.

Example: An experience of great loss that leaves a tear in the area of the heart. This person will suffer from leaking healthy heart energy – depletion in that area, as well as a weak, extremely vulnerable state of grief. This vulnerable auric shield may make them susceptible to an invasive, off-balance emotion that is replacing the lost love, but not in an entirely healthy way.

Example: Perhaps a state of extreme neediness, helplessness, and overall lack of self-esteem has left a person very depleted and weak. This may attract the opposite. An unbalanced energy source that tends to overwhelm, control and bully, may find its way into the auric tear and overpower the vulnerable person with their unhealthy, overwhelming and possessively imposing dynamic.

THE NEW NORMAL

The unfortunate aspect in PTSD is the last word – disorder. It creates a perception of something that is damaged, with an element of dis-function, perhaps even shame, that something is not working properly. It describes the trauma in a way that indicates one has suffered damage, they are out of order – remaining in a state of disorder. And since we are always encouraged and expected to be perfect, this immediately establishes a state of unworthiness.

But quite the opposite is true. The reality is, that most of us suffer from some form of PTSD, some smaller some bigger, it's simply a fact of life.

WE HAVE ALL ENDURED EXPERIENCES WHICH LEFT REPERCUSSIONS.

All of us have most likely had difficult experiences. That is simply a part of life. And as I mentioned before, the question is: how much can you withstand? What are the aftereffects for you, individually? As our levels of tolerance differ, it is impossible to measure trauma and the after-effects it leaves on our overall system. When promoting the psychological aspect of healing, it would be more positive to address PTSD as a temporary energy weakened state that can be overcome, and in time transformed into a beneficial asset.

Of course that may not be possible in all cases, and often we simply cannot completely overcome the after-effects and some PTSD remains. However, the symptoms can be greatly improved, possibly almost entirely eliminated, but certainly effectively reduced and properly managed, so that PTSD does not continue to affect our lives in a negative way. The aftereffects of trauma create for us a new state of normal. We adjust, we shift, our perception is leaning heavily into a negative, or fearful direction. This is unpleasant and dangerous, because it alters our sense of reality. We may actually begin convincing ourselves that the traumatic situation is the new normal. Or that the aftereffects of trauma which linger in our energy body, have altered our life in such a way, that we accept it as our new state of normal.

A dramatic example would be with people who are victims of war crimes, or some other extremely violent act. In the aftereffects of these occurrences, the PTSD may manifest itself in the form of emotional numbness. Once such violence is witnessed, nothing seems to affect the person anymore, as nothing measures against what they have witnessed. These are the most challenging cases. Can such cases improve and find some kind of normalcy? With time, and depending on the individual resilience and subtle energy natural state of each individual. The emotional numbness can of course happen with any kind of trauma, but to a lesser degree. It can also happen simply from a strictly sensory perspective. The more our senses are abused or exposed to unhealthy dosage of overstimulation, the bigger the possibility, that we succumb to a state of numbness, and are unable to register or process sensory information in a normal and fully effective way. From the esoteric perspective, the emotional numbness is like a state of frozen and stuck energy congestion.

If we cannot connect to our emotional state, we are suffering from out of balance interaction between our subtle energy layers. This can express itself as an overload of mental activity, or unbalanced physical behavior. The balance between all our subtle energy layers has to be finely tuned and reciprocally supportive. If it is not, the imbalance can manifest itself in countless unharmonious ways.

PTSD MUST BE ADDRESSED HOLISTICALLY FROM ALL ASPECTS: PHYSICAL, MENTAL AND EMOTIONAL BALANCE CAN BE STIMULATED WITH CONSCIOUS APPLICATION OF PROPER HEALING MODALITIES.

ADJUSTED PERCEPTIONS

The way our perception will shift after trauma, is that we may be talking ourselves into believing that the difficult state is normal, and the new dysfunction is our new natural state. We see life through the prism of our traumatic event. In physically painful cases, we will assume that the pain can and will be repeated. In mentally challenging cases, we will expect the same mental pain to be inflicted. And in emotional aspects, we will anticipate that this is the way everyone and everything functions. We expect the worst, therefore we live in a perpetual state of preparedness. This is extremely draining and hard to sustain. When your perspective field shifts, so does your belief system, the vision of your future and the span of possibilities. We carry the wound, but try to ignore it. We live with the wound, and suspect we shall never function properly again, like we did before the trauma. This new and very limited perception or fear induced PTSD perception, can be healed through an actively multi layered sensory healing process. In other words, we need to engage all aspects of our being, the physical, mental, and emotional side of our personality. All our aspects need to have an opportunity to express and release the pain, and consciously create space for new positive input of information that overrides and annuls the damaging and negative information.

HIDDEN TRAUMA EFFECTS ON YOUR PHYSICAL BODY

Obviously there are many forms of possible physical trauma. But here we are focusing on non-physical trauma – the aftereffects of emotional or mental trauma that resides solely in the subtle energy field. But even non-physical trauma with long term infliction, can in time manifest signs of physical distress and illness in your physical body. Such trauma can affect any area of your physical body, and will express itself in the chakra area that corresponds to the nature of the problem you have endured or are still suffering through.

For example; if for years you have suffered emotional and mental abuse in a relationship, your energy body will deteriorate. You may not have any physical wounds to show, but your subtle energy body will endure invisible injury. This traumatic subtle energy damage will eventually turn into physical ailments or disease. In this case, the areas most vulnerable to manifesting physical illness would be your heart, breasts and lungs – in connection to grief and emotional expression. In case of physical relationships that are emotionally abusive, your sexual and reproductive organs are energetically also very vulnerable. This does not differ in male or female victim, but more often, the female is on the receiving end of the traumatic dynamic. In another case of traumatic mental overstimulation as in a restless mind, overthinking in obsessive recall of traumatic experience could manifest itself in physical ailments of head, brain, hearing, sight and neurological disorders.

TRAUMA REVERBERATION ON THE WAY YOU THINK – YOUR MENTAL BODY

A traumatic event can cause great suffering to your ethereal mental body – this is the field that carries your thought patterns, your mental disposition, your perpetual inner dialogue. The negative traumatic patterns can remain in one's mindset and way of thinking, and negatively affect every area of their life. Mind disposition has a great importance on overall quality of life. Past trauma may affect you in a way you may not even notice, as a subtle but persistent permeation and anticipation of perpetual disappointment or mental pain. In such a case, the person would always assume the worst-case scenario, refuse to verbalize their expectations in fear of not having them met, and mentally project only negative and disturbing events in their possible future. They would create a mental block that would affect all other subtle energy layers and would manifest in emotional unavailability, physical

stagnation, and overall mental incapacity to open up to new patterns, positive input and changes that would help one move from status quo, into progress and new possibilities. They will resist connecting with new people and remain in their mentally stagnant 'safe-zone' without realizing, that it is precisely this habit that will keep them locked in their PTSD negative pattern.

TRAUMA IMPACT ON THE WAY YOU FEEL — YOUR EMOTIONAL BODY

The trauma after-effects on emotional body can be quite complex. This can express itself in the way one communicates and interacts with others. The most traumatic aftereffects will manifest in personal relationships, as this is where emotional openness and receptivity is most required. Emotional expression will be out of balance, possibly unexpectedly swinging in either direction. It may express itself as extremely closed-off disposition, stubborn silence, verbal abuse, passive aggression, demeaning and self-depriving, self-loathing, or the total opposite. They might be overextending, never stating their true needs or wishes, tolerating anything imposed upon them, quietly suffering, and actually unknowingly helping to sustain another continuous abusive relationship. The lack of self-worth would keep them in perpetual state of self-blame. Such unharmonious state will reverberate through the emotional body and affect all other energy layers of their being.

TRAUMA CONSEQUENCES ON YOUR SUBTLE ENERGY BODY

The assessed sum total of various causes and residuals of your old or recent trauma, is obviously encoded into your subtle body. In fact, this is where it may be present without any visible physical, emotional or mental signs. This is why it is very important for you to explore, self-analyze and discover all those intricate, complex and perhaps forgotten events that shaped your state of resilience, as well as vulnerability in your life. Once you recognize the aftereffects, you can consciously release them. The biggest, most complex work, is the actual self-realization. Once the trauma is exposed, you will experience a deep personal transformation as the release process begins. It will feel like you are peeling an onion – layers upon layers will reveal themselves, each time releasing a burden you are ready to recognize and discard. When you come to this point, you are ready to begin incorporating healing modalities that will help you re-establish a new, healthy and strong subtle energy body. It has a natural ability to regenerate in most amazing ways, but only after you release congestion, pollution and unnecessary energy concentration that does not serve your higher soul interest. You have to release the old, in order to make space for the new.

YOUR ASSIGNMENT

AFFIRMATION

THE POWER AND MY ABILITY TO REGENERATE IS MY GREATEST ASSET

DIARY

In this chapter you are learning to recognize and analyze the patterns of your wound. The better you understand the details, the faster your healing process will begin. Identify the connection between your current life trauma and examine your childhood trauma residuals and how that affects your life today.

When did you experience most challenging years? How did that affect you?

What residuals of that event can you find in your life today?

Step by step reclaim your power, by recognizing and releasing the unpleasant memory with focusing on the courageous, strong part of your personality, that emerged resilient and victorious. Focus on the positive – wisdom and abilities gained from your past experience.

PROCESS

Work thru the questions, come back in a few days, see if anything changed, add it on, clarify and self-discover through the process.

PRACTICE

This week you will continue with the journaling process and begin with the first Mudra. The Mudra practice should be your opportunity to establish an easy, time effective daily new routine that will expand with time. Become bonded with the new state of peace and serenity that the Mudra evokes, and enjoy the stillness – the sacred inner field of no burdens, thoughts or stress. Your soul is untouchable and forever connected to the Universe. With each breath, feel and reestablish this connection. Write down your thoughts and reflections. Affirm for yourself, that your healing process has begun and your delicate energy field is mending.

**THE SELF - HEALING PROCESS HAS BEGUN.
YOU KNOW THE SOURCE AND LOCATION OF YOUR WOUND.
PREPARE TO RELEASE THE OLD BURDEN AND SOAR.**

TRACES OF TRAUMA IN YOUR BEING

1. ARE YOU IN PHYSICAL PAIN? WHERE?

CONNECT IT TO THE NEAREST CHAKRA CENTER.

EXAMINE YOUR PAST AND CURRENT TRAUMA IN CONNECTION WITH THAT CHAKRA.

2. ARE YOU IN EMOTIONAL PAIN?

CONNECT IT TO THE CORRESPONDING CHAKRA CENTER— ANGER, LOVE, TRUST?

EXAMINE YOUR PAST AND CURRENT TRAUMA IN CONNECTION WITH THAT CHAKRA.

3. ARE YOU IN MENTAL PAIN?

CONNECT IT TO THE CORRESPONDING CHAKRA CENTER, IN LOWER 3 CHAKRAS.

EXAMINE YOUR PAST AND CURRENT TRAUMA IN CONNECTION WITH THAT CHAKRA.

LAUNCHING THE HEALING PROCESS
WITH MUDRAS

This week we begin with this basic Mudra, to help you regain inner equilibrium. This is the first step to take a pause, get centered, and begin to re-establish your core energy vibration.

Reclaiming your absolute presence and awareness will help you merge your subtle energy fields that may be disproportionately unharmonious, as a result of your specific unique trauma aftereffects. Merging your body, mind and spirit, will recreate the healthy auric shield pattern, that is naturally resilient and impenetrable.

Your cells remember the seed information of healthy functioning, and now you will remind your being to re-establish this healthy rhythm, and the self-healing process will begin.

Practice this Mudra three minutes every day, first thing in the morning and last thing in the evening. Remain disciplined with this daily practice and observe a new, yet pleasantly familiar feeling of inner peace that will envelop your physical body, still your mind, and soothe your heart.

MUDRA for DEVELOPING MEDITATION

Sit with a straight back and keep your shoulders down, nice and relaxed. Hold the left palm open and facing the sky. Lift up your hands to the level of solar plexus and place the four fingers of the right hand on your left wrist to feel your pulse. Pressing lightly, the fingers of the right hand are positioned nicely in a straight line on the wrist of the left hand. Concentrate and completely focus on your pulse. Hands and elbows are away from body. With each pulse-beat, repeat the mantra Sat Nam. After a minute, practice without mantra and expand your awareness to connect with the Universal heartbeat. Continue for Three minutes and relax.

BREATH
LONG, DEEP AND SLOW THRU YOUR NOSE
MANTRA
SAT NAM *(Truth is God's name, One in Spirit)*
AFFIRMATION

I AM ONE WITH THE UNIVERSE

Week Three

RECOGNIZE YOUR PATTERNS

No child is born with a generally negative attitude towards life. They may be sensitive, delicate, easily fearful, but they are not negatively inclined. They are not hostile from the get-go. They come into this life mostly enthusiastic, open and optimistic about a new adventure. They look at the world curiously, interested in everything that surrounds them.

We are born without immediate memory of our last life and even in cases where children do remember a past life, they don't remember the sadness, or horror, or tragedy. If they do, it is very detached, almost reflective in a way. That memory is veiled in distance and the fog of reincarnation forgetfulness. This is how you have an opportunity for a new, fresh, enthusiastic beginning. Whatever happens to you from day one onwards, affects you and shapes your understanding, experience, and disposition towards this world, life and people in it.

PTSD FROM YOUR FAR PAST LEAVES CERTAIN ENTRAINED PATTERNS, BUT AS A NEWBORN HUMAN, YOU ARE HOPEFUL ABOUT YOUR DREAMS.

All options lie on the table. This is why children have big dreams, and teenagers have hopeful wishes about their life when they'll grow up. They can't wait. And adults often give up on dreams, or dream only secretly. If the early years of human life are filled with trauma, upheaval, distress, or tragedy, this basic hope and enthusiasm is tainted, often completely lost. Suddenly the hopeful future becomes the dreaded hopeless future.

What to do? The resilient ones persist, fight, and overcome the obstacles, and the less supported ones fall pray to negative routes. There is always a possibility that you will find your way back onto the correct path, but equally so, the possibility of getting permanently lost, exists. These life paths reveal the magnitude of the damaging effects a trauma has had on our life.

There is no one to blame. Yes, you can find reasons, culprits, but this is life. Some of us have a destiny that's more challenging than others. Some of us are faced with indescribable challenges, and difficulties. How we overcome them, manage them, and diffuse their effects on the rest of our lives, depends on so many factors. Nevertheless, here we are – the sum total of what's happened to us, up to this very minute. This leaves us with certain patterns, preexisting habits, and inclinations.

What seems most challenging, the thing we avoid the most shall come back to haunt us. Sooner or later we will have to figure it out, and face it head-on. Escape in this case will not work. Escaping life's challenges never works.

ESCAPING CONSEQUENCES OF OUR ACTIONS, IS NOT THE WAY THE UNIVERSE WORKS.

You may escape dangers, bad decisions, unfortunate accidents that maybe happened by chance, or sheer bad luck. But your past and its consequences are part of your Soul journey and need to be healed, re-established, and reconfigured in time.

The only question is…how much time? When is the best time to do damage control? Usually the answer is: NOW. If you can't manage it now, then there's always the next lifetime, but rest assured, the challenge shall return until you conquer it, and find a way to deal with it, in a way that is less consequential. You simply have to overcome it. It is part of your evolutionary process.

All this brings us to the topic of patterns.
What are your daily patters that affect your general quality of life?
Here we are going to review patterns that are a direct result of a past trauma.
For reviewing this concept we will touch on SEVEN important aspects - connected to the seven chakras.

CHAKRA PATTERNS AND PTSD

If a past trauma negatively affected your disposition towards survival, how does this pattern reflect, or show up in your everyday life? This is very important, because being stuck in an old PTSD pattern, will not create an ideal circumstance for you to change, shift and move on with your life.

A PAST-LIFE PTSD PATTERN WILL KEEP YOU HOSTAGE.

CHAKRA I.

If you find yourself in perpetual survival mode, your entire life will revolve around that one aspect. You will see people, events, locations and situations through the prism of — how can this help you survive?

This kind of pattern completely disturbs your objective observation of your environment and people in it. You may connect with or pursue people you would otherwise not, simply because you are in fear for your own survival and therefore your pattern is to associate only with people that may benefit you in some way or another. This is one example of a PTSD pattern connected to chakra one.

Shifting this pattern will require your clear awareness, that you are stuck in a PTSD triggered habit. Next, you have to consciously overcome the fear-based limitations of your mind. If you believe that the only way to survive, is to get help from somewhere or someone else outside of yourself, you will look in vain.

WAITING TO BE RESCUED IS NOT A HEALTHY ANSWER.
IT IS A RATHER POWERLESS ACT OF DESPERATION.

In a healthy pattern you will be aware that you can pull yourself out of this negative financial pattern, and overcome the survival mode. This realization has the potential to completely change your life. Some people remain in a survival pattern regardless how much wealth they have. They still fear the repeat of the same event that traumatized them in the past. This was often the case with victims of war that endured tremendous hardships with their life in constant danger, perhaps barely existing with nothing to eat, or no place to be safe. Such a person would suffer from PTSD even if they recovered financially, and would always remain extremely fearful of letting go of money, going hungry, because they remain stuck in the old traumatic pattern. A homeless person, or someone who lost their home due to natural disaster or economic upheaval, may carry a pattern of expecting to lose the home again, in whatever traumatic way they did before. This PTSD will follow them and affect all areas of their life and choices they make. This pattern associated with Chakra I. will also indirectly affect all other chakras, because if you don't feel stable, secure, and safe in the world, it becomes very challenging to build all other aspects of existence with confidence and an optimistic disposition.

The PTSD pattern after a disruptive event connected with Chakra I. will remain, no matter how one's life circumstances improve. If a person is aware and resilient, they will overcome this PTSD pattern and recover with the ability to embrace a new, positive, supportive and safe environment, that they hopefully regain later in life. They will be able to enjoy it, truly relax in it, and eliminate the survival mode behavior. This will completely change their life, in a most positive way. Their interaction with others will be healthier and more harmonious.

CHAKRA II. pattern will have to do with your creative expression and sexual interaction. PTSD patterns following a traumatic event that is connected to Chakra II. will leave the person in a certain expectation mode, that everything in the future will be similarly traumatic, just as they experienced it during the past trauma. If a person is a victim of physical violence, rape, or any kind of sexual trauma, this will leave them with a pattern of great fear, aversion and resistance to trusting and letting to.

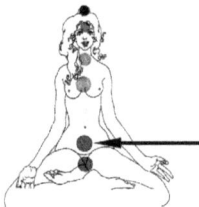

This will create an energy block, an impenetrable wall between the physical aspect of sexual interaction and healthy emotional connection. Detachment from physical experience or fear of enjoyment, guilt, weak self-confidence, all these complex issues will arise and interrupt a healthy flow of energy. An example of patterns connected with creative expression would be, if someone was criticized in a damaging way, prevented from expressing their creativity, or punished for their creative expression. This will become a serious energy block, that will negatively affect all energy centers, the closest centers being Chakra I. and Chakra III. This is where the damaging patterns will spill over and leave after-effects.

For example: in connection to Chakra I. follow up after-effects from Chakra II. trauma, the person would have a very hard time feeling secure, safe, or may associate sexuality strictly connected to security. As a result, they may abuse or be abused in connecting these two aspects, as if they are interdependent with each other. In the upwards direction to Chakra

III., the Chakra II. PTSD pattern may negatively affect the person to express great anger, violence, ego imbalance, or obsessive mind behavior, connected to sexuality or creative expression.

CHAKRA III. pattern may express itself with imbalanced ego or overactive mind, and obsessive habits. If someone experiences great trauma in connection to their Chakra III, the PTSD pattern may express itself through ego-maniac, narcissist behavior, extreme pride, anger, violence, deep insecurity, bullying and otherwise obsessive and imbalanced-mind behavior. The subtle energy after-effects will spill over to Chakra II. area, and could create violence connected to sexuality, or feeling the need to express creativity through anger, aggression, in a generally negative direction. If the Chakra III. PTSD spills over into Chakra IV., this will affect their ability to express love or properly function in a healthy relationship. Their heart will confuse love with acts of anger and perpetual fear.

CHAKRA IV. pattern main subject is about love and how one functions in relationships. If they experienced a very traumatic love relationship, great loss, massive wound, betrayal, or otherwise distressing love experience, they will carry perpetual fear of associating love with pain and loss. This may create a PTSD pattern of not allowing themselves to open up to a new relationship, trust anyone, and a permanent expectancy that if they open to love, they will be betrayed, forgotten, left behind, abandoned and will relive their previous trauma. This kind of PTSD is very common and it can be overcome, but only with conscious participation of the victim. If the negative PTSD pattern from Chakra IV. spills over to Chakra III., they will associate love with aggression, mind control, imbalanced ego behavior, reasoning, and logical justifications in the mind. This is a losing battle, as mind cannot control your heart. This pattern will also affect Chakra V. in a way, that the person will not be able to speak the truth. Therefore their expression of love will be lost in untruth, dishonesty, punishing silence, and unhealthy communication. This behavior is the ripple effect pattern from Chakra IV. PTSD. They may be able to give love only under very specific conditions, bargaining and negotiating what should come naturally. The PTSD pattern of the heart matters will be repeated in all relationships, until the person recognizes and overcomes it, and consciously opens up to a positive transformation.

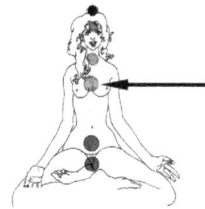

CHAKRA V. If the PTSD pattern is connected to Chakra V. area, the ability to communicate will be negatively affected. Perhaps the person was punished in the past for speaking up, or speaking their mind, or simply speaking the truth. This leaves them with a PTSD pattern of fearing to express themselves in any way. The negative effects of this pattern will prevent them from being able to express their feelings of love - Chakra IV. or find their own intuitive answers through Chakra VI.

CHAKRA VI. If the PTSD pattern is stuck in Chakra VI. as a result of an experience where their intuition was mistaken or caused great trauma, this person will live with the PTSD ripple effect manifested as an inability to trust their own intuition – or anyone else's, for that matter. They will suffer from feeling betrayal, error, superstition, belief in invisible punishment, and consequentially making the wrong choices. The damaging PTSD pattern spilling into Chakra V. would manifest as an inability to communicate their intuitive feelings, hesitancy to speak their ideas, suggestions or solutions. They will be stuck in PTSD pattern of resisting, feeling lost, and remain fearful of speaking their mind.

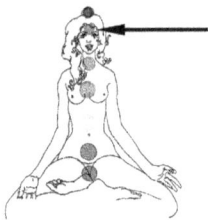

CHAKRA VII. And finally, in expanding to Chakra VII. the PTSD damaging pattern will manifest in the person doubting the presence of higher power, while they suffer from feeling utter abandonment, isolation and hopelessness. Negative experiences connected to matters of Chakra VII. will leave a PTSD pattern of religion-based feelings of loss, or betrayal they might have lived through in the far-away past or current life. They will doubt Divine protection, Divine rights and fear karmic punishment. If Chakra VII. associated PTSD patterns spills over towards Chakra VI. center, the person will not trust their own intuition of Divine expression or self-realization, they will have a distorted view of Divinity and their own higher consciousness.

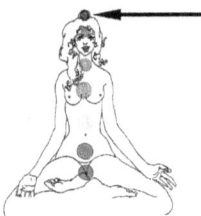

HOW ARE YOU DEALING WITH PAIN?

There are many kinds of pain, some on purely subtle level and invisible to others. The way you acknowledge, recognize and deal with pain, can be connected to your PTSD pattern as it relates to Chakras.

For example: Fear for survival is connected with PTSD Chakra I. issue. Fear of creative or sexual expression is connected with PTSD from Chakra II. area, and so on.

Why are these connections important?
They give you an opportunity to heal your PTSD from the subtle energy perspective of Chakras. This makes it much clearer what areas of your life are connected and suffering from PTSD after-effects.

For example: if your trauma has to do with sexual abuse, this will affect your relationships, self-confidence, expression and intuition in that order, but the worst ripple effects will be with Chakra I. and Chakra III. since they are the closest chakras to Chakra II. area – the actual source of PTSD.

If you pain has to do with heart – loss of love or betrayal, the PTSD will manifest in not trusting or communicating – Chakra V. connection – and feeling anger and fear – Chakra III. connection – and much less with actual creative or sexual expression.

Such a person could have a very active sexual life, that would be entirely void of love, or similar emotions. They would feel anger, fear and not speak their truth. It is important to understand and recognize these subtle energy principles. Certainly the possibilities are endless, but understanding this concept will help you take proper steps to re-establish a healthy balance.

THE KEY IS RECOGNIZING IN WHICH OF YOUR CHAKRAS LIES THE MAIN SOURCE OF YOUR PTSD.

DENIAL AND ESCAPE

If your PTSD pattern is denial and escape, it means that the traumatic event is obscured with so much fear, that you are subconsciously attempting to block it out of your system, and are pretending it never happened. Of course this cannot be something indefinitely sustained, as subtle energy resides in the energy layers of your entire body and lingers there, possibly for a very long time. In fact, time does not matter. A certain powerful trigger could unexpectedly bring back the traumatic experience, and all the denial in the world would not help you.

The therapeutic approach to overcome this pattern is to catch the trigger, observe it and recognize it. The moment your trigger is identified, you can begin to overpower it.

WHAT YOU KNOW, YOU CAN CONQUER.
WHAT'S INVISIBLE, YOU CAN'T OVERPOWER.

Recognizing why a certain trigger may hold such power over you, will require exploring your past and remembering a similar event that evoked the same feelings.

For example: if a traumatic break-up is your source of PTSD, it may be triggered every time a very similar partnership or relationship dynamic comes your way. If your previous partner that is connected to the traumatic experience was of a certain profession, had certain physical attributes, habits or unique traits, every time that a new potential partner demonstrates a similarity, you may be triggered and run the other way, expecting and assuming the worst – a repeated trauma. Your PTSD is preventing you from moving forward and opening to the possibility of a new, healthy relationship. If you live in denial and are unaware of your PTSD, you can pretend all this is not happening. OR you can face it, and see that it is just a similarity, which doesn't mean at all, that the new partner is going to behave like the one before. They may possess certain similarities, but are in fact different.

Another example would be if you have had a traumatic experience with loss of safety, security, possessions or work. Your PTSD will linger within your emotional body permeated with persistent fear of experiencing a repeated trauma. If you lost your house, you may fear it will happen again. If you lost a job, you will fear you are likely to lose the next job again. If you've lost all your money and worldly possessions, you will most likely live in fear that it will happen again. Or you will live with PTSD of desperately trying to recreate what you once had, when in fact you should move forward, do things differently than in the past, and rediscover your new life that awaits. In all these cases PTSD holds you captive in a cloud of fear, that prevents you from moving forward or opening up to the possibility that your life will improve. You expect the worst and dread each new coming day, but refuse to admit it – this is living in denial. This kind of permanent emotional pressure is often very challenging and prevents us from functioning normally. People begin to look for other ways of escaping the hidden emotional pressure of PTSD. Unfortunately, quite often, they will escape beyond denial into the world of addiction and further dysfunction.

THE MANY SHADES OF ADDICTION

This is a very complex challenge and I could write a whole book on this difficult and extensive topic. Addiction is in fact very closely connected to PTSD and most often the immediate consequence of a traumatic event in someone's life. It is important to touch on it partially here on our PTSD healing journey, so you understand all consequences that play an important role.

We need to recognize that the world of addiction has many different categories and areas of manifestation, but the intention is usually the same or very similar – to escape from reality while numbing your senses from pain, and distancing yourself from whatever is causing you emotional, mental or physical suffering.

PTSD IS THE PRIMARY REASON FOR THE DESIRE TO ESCAPE REALITY.

If someone's everyday life is unbearable, while they are facing an overwhelming situation, they will feel the immediate and desperate need to numb their senses in order to be able to bear it. They can't face the raw reality. It needs to be dissolved into a less potent state. The unfortunate dynamic is, that while numbing their senses to escape from pain, they are magnifying the unhealthy state of suffering and distancing themselves from a healthy natural functioning. It will be even more difficult to recover and heal from PTSD, if one has succumbed to addiction and is even more distanced from their true feelings.

When PTSD suffering expands into addictive or self-destructive behavior pattern, the problematic scope grows. While we usually imagine addiction in connection to drugs or alcohol, there are of course incredibly complex addictions, such as abusive relationships, co-dependence, self-destructive behavior of different kinds, overeating, social media and electronics, sugar, shopping…to name a few. But it all turns again into patterns that follow a PTSD triggered episode. Changing and eliminating these destructive patterns is something that depends on the individual's willingness, willpower, and true desire to overcome a particular addiction. Strong and professional support systems are needed to help you overcome the persistent urge to escape into addiction, whatever the nature of it is. It would be more constructive and effective to truly look at PTSD and all the intricate details that are involved, before looking at addictions as a separate matter. The interconnected way of healing any unharmonious states is to always look at the whole scope of human experience.

> **ONCE WE CLEARLY RECOGNIZE THE CAUSE AND NATURE OF PTSD, WE CAN ADDRESS THE ADDICTIVE PATTERNS THAT HAVE EMERGED.**

It is impossible to overcome addictive tendencies, if we ignore the important role of PTSD as the main cause of the addiction. Once we address PTSD, an open healing energy field is established and we can begin recognizing and hopefully eliminating the patterns of addictive behavior. Quite often a person may not be aware of the PTSD source, they only register that they are in pain and wish to escape the suffering. Once they recognize the underlying cause, they can begin healing, mending, overcoming and forgiving whatever caused their PTSD. They feel more empowered, aware, and less of a helpless victim. They have the opportunity to reclaim their own power. This is of significant importance. From the esoteric perspective, the PTSD energy congestion escalates and creates a significant subtle energy imbalance, that causes a depleted state in the energy center associated with the consequential addiction. They feel the need to artificially replace the void in the affected energy field with a substance, that will help artificially maintain a sense of balance. Addiction is a temporary fix, trying to arrest PTSD. It won't work.

SELF-ABUSE, A CRY FOR HELP

This is a form of PTSD that manifests as a consequence and persists in this form of silent suffering, where a person does not have the ability to express their emotions, inner pain, insecurities or debilitating fear that overwhelms their entire life. This challenging state completely conceals their life purpose and a person gets lost in a maze of depressive, secluded, secretive and self-harming behavior pattern. Addictive behavior is self-destructive, as is this manifestation of PTSD. But quite often the person suffering does not recognize or see it that way.

Again, the main cause of PTSD has to be discovered before healing can begin. Often this pattern will emerge after trauma connected to abandonment issues, self-esteem challenges, or extreme societal expectations from the individual, for instance with fame, physical perfection, or constant delivery of creative genius. Finding the cause is the first step to beginning the healing process.

ATTRACTING FAMILIAR DYNAMICS

This is a well known fact – as I have written in my books, such as *Mudra Therapy*, the beginning childhood dynamics are a great indicator of our future challenges. If one suffered a difficult childhood with many traumatic events, chances are that their PTSD will manifest as an inherent dysfunction, and they will subconsciously seek out, feel attracted to, or follow a pattern that they were brought up with, and experienced in their childhood.

If one parent suffered from PTSD which manifested in their own addictive and abusive behavior dynamics, the pattern is set, and the PTSD consequence will likely manifest in the child – now a grown person, who will continue the PTSD patterns. The now adult person will simply expect all their future relationships will present themselves in an identical picture to their parent's dynamic. This of course does not have to be so, and can absolutely be changed and overcome, but the first immediate reaction and tendency will be, to assume that this is the normal dynamic, and therefore one must learn how to live with it and tolerate it. They may even have a difficult time functioning in a normal healthy relationship, simply because they never witnessed it, or participated in one.

This is a generational PTSD pattern that will follow the person until they recognize it and consciously shift the dynamic.

Can it be done? Absolutely. Is it easy? It requires determination, awareness, willpower and discipline to consciously create a different, healthier future for yourself. Soul searching and self-awareness are the key. Then, it becomes an avalanche of released power and incredible feeling of freedom, as you throw away the handcuffs of the past and become you own person.

YOU CAN CREATE A NEW, HEALTHY AND LOVING REALITY AND LIFE THAT SUITS YOU AND NOT YOUR PAST EXAMPLES.

REPEATING THE PATTERN

I t is easiest to do what you know, it is demanding to stretch yourself out of the comfort zone and change things, especially if your personality is more subdued and you prefer to live in a routine. However, there comes a time where you need to recognize what is simply healthy or unhealthy. The difference is of decisive importance.

Once you have tasted the healthy, loving, kind and self-respecting experience of life, it will be impossible to tolerate the old dysfunctional behavior. PTSD will push you into following the old patterns, but getting to the source of your PTSD will prompt an energy reaction, that will make it impossible to sustain or ignore. It is human nature to want to improve, feel happy and loved. This will never go away. Once you recognize that this experience is a possibility if you open up to it, chances are you will be able to overcome the old, dysfunctional patterns and establish a new pattern that is healthy, peaceful, creative and filled with self-respect, kindness and love.

Interaction with others is your greatest indicator of all behavioral tendencies. We are meant to communicate, enjoy personal relationships, friendships, and this is what every human needs in order to function in a healthy, satisfied way. Changing your pattern is possible, once PTSD is addressed and you are ready to embrace a new life you choose, not what was chosen for you by your predecessors, or anyone else. When you are ready, you will cease repeating the old patterns.

LONG AGO DOESN'T MEAN GONE

If your trauma happened many years or even lifetimes ago, it has not vanished into the ether, therefore it is important to keep in mind and observe any patterns that you have now, and recognize their connection to something in this or previous life. Patterns repeat themselves, often even generationally. PTSD patterns become karmic patterns, deeply engrained into our psyche and energy subtle body. Karmic patterns can be broken, but with time they become such a familiar and intricate part of yourself, that it requires extra strength and a clear intention to release, shift and eliminate them. You are in the best position of overcoming unwelcome old or new patterns when you embark on the journey of self-discovery, as you are doing now.

Your life will only become what you wish, once you completely know and understand your very delicate nuances that make you the unique individual that you are.

THE LINGERING EFFECTS

After you recognize the pattern and consciously begin to shift your perspective and behavioral tendencies, you will notice the lingering after-effects in your subtle energy body. In other words, your normal, usual reflex will be to react in certain ways to triggers or any kind of situations, where your PTSD is engrained into your psyche. The lingering effect will be present for a long time, but will eventually weaken and become more of a realization and a reminder of what you have overcome and what tremendous progress you have made in your evolutionary self-freeing and healing journey. The lingering effects are not bad, but actually a great gift, because they help you find a clear way out of the old maze you aimlessly wandered. It is almost as if you have an opportunity to do a comparative study of yourself. This was you before, and this is you now. It will help you stay on track to complete recovery work from PTSD, and develop an entirely different perspective. Older memories may emerge that will make even more sense, and you will uncover other details that matter in your healing process.

THERE IS NO REASON TO FEAR YOUR SELF-HEALING JOURNEY.

The past is the past and now, this very moment, you are untouchable. Just remember, you are moving forward, out of the old and into the new.

WALKING IN CIRCLES

If you find yourself walking in circles and not making the progress that you desire, ask yourself which fear keeps you in the state of hesitation and is preventing you from moving forward? Be direct and clear with your self-examination, and you will find deeper clarity and profound resolve, to leave behind whatever held you in the stagnant pattern. Once you begin breaking your stagnation, and chip it away piece by piece, a great self-confidence building mechanism will emerge as you witness, in your own time, with your own eyes, the progress you've made, and how much better and freer your life has become. This is a very private and intimate journey within yourself. You are the driver, you are the deciding voice, and you have the final say how you wish to see, use and process the PTSD that you've lived with. Slowly but surely your PTSD will become an empowering experience, that will expand your awareness into an amazing field of perception you never imagined.

YOUR ASSIGNMENT

AFFIRMATION

MY NEW PATTERNS WILL CREATE WAVES OF PEACE

DIARY

In this chapter you are recognizing and analyzing any and all patterns that may be following you through generations, or that you picked up through your life's various experiences. This is a very crucial step in unraveling and dissolving the limiting, restrictive and energy draining grip PTSD may have on your subconscious. Patterns are like various templates that repeat themselves, quite predictably. Once you recognize them, you can begin to weaken and eventually dismantle them. As a result, you are able to predict, manage and effectively overcome your PTSD. The more you examine the details, the faster you can defeat this undesirable dynamic and regain your optimal balance and harmony.

PROCESS

Work thru the questions, come back in a few days, see if anything changed, add it on, clarify and self-discover through the process.

PRACTICE

This week is about self-exploration and finding patterns. Make a conscious effort to find obstructive PTSD patterns that follow you through life. Write them down and keep researching and adding anything that may help you see the bigger integrated picture. Practice the Mudras and observe the difference in your emotional and mental state, before and after you work through these self-discovery steps. What you'll find at the end of this exploration, will help you shed light on many past events and choices. You will find clarity, and perhaps even some logic. All of these realizations will help you towards the next step that awaits in the coming chapter – how to release the burdens of your past.

YOUR PATTERNS CREATED THE FABRIC OF YOUR PAST.
CHANGE THEM AND CREATE YOUR NEW FUTURE.
IT IS IN YOUR HANDS.

FIND YOUR PATTERN

1. IS THERE A FAMILY PTSD PATTERN OF YOUR MOTHER THAT YOU ARE REPEATING?

2. IS THERE A FAMILY PTSD PATTERN OF YOUR FATHER THAT YOU ARE REPEATING?

3. ARE YOUR EMOTIONAL, MENTAL OR BELIEF PATTERNS FOLLOWING YOUR PARENT'S OR RELATIVE'S EXAMPLE?

4. HAVE YOU MANAGED TO BREAK SOME OF THE UNDESIRABLE PATTERNS?

5. WHAT PATTERN IS MOST CHALLENGING FOR YOU?

6. DO YOU HAVE ANY ADDICTIVE, SELF-LIMITING, OR SELF-SABOTAGING PATTERNS?

7. ARE YOU MAKING CONSCIOUS EFFORT TO CHANGE YOUR LESS DESIRABLE PATTERNS?

8. WHICH OF YOUR ENERGY CENTERS - CHAKRAS IS MOST BURDENED WITH PATTERNS?

9. WHICH OF YOUR CHAKRAS IS MOST POWERFUL AND FUNCTIONS AT OPTIMUM?

MUDRA FOR EMOTIONAL BALANCE

Examining your old patterns, discovering what you've been unconsciously dragging along, and inherited challenges, can trigger vulnerable and reactive emotional states. This is a normal and welcome part of the process, because you are recognizing the issues, the sources and can finally clear them out of your energy body's delicate field of information.

This Mudra is excellent for balancing emotional states and learning to comfort yourself quickly and effectively, for long-term. It is an empowering step in your healing process to learn self-reliance, and recognize that you are not helpless, but rather victorious, empowered and perfectly capable of overcoming the undesirable effects of the past, and prevent them from following you into present and the future.

You are in charge. You are the command center of your emotional state. By breathing calm, long, deep and slow you will balance your emotions and suddenly realize that everything can be perfectly harmonious, yourself included, IF and WHEN you balance your emotions. You recognize and acknowledge them, but you don't let them overcome you with such force that they rob you of your peace.

Work with your emotions and a counterbalanced harmony will become your welcome and healthy routine.

CHAKRAS
All Chakras

HEALING COLORS
All Colors

AFFIRMATION

I AM IN PERFECT BALANCE, MY HEART IS PEACEFUL

Before this practice, drink a glass of water to balance your system. Sit with a straight back and keep your shoulders down, nice and relaxed. Place the hands flat against your body, under each armpit and wrap your hands around your body as if giving yourself a hug. Keep your palms open. Close your eyes, take a deep inhale, give yourself a strong hug and lift your shoulders towards your ears and lower your head for a few moments. Hold your breath, then exhale while lowering your shoulders, lifting your head and loosening the embrace. Continue for Three minutes, then relax.

BREATH
LONG, DEEP AND SLOW THRU YOUR NOSE

MANTRA
SAT NAM *(Truth is God's Name)*

MUDRA for MENTAL BALANCE

Now that you've reflected upon the many complex nuances of various patterns and how they can manifest, carry over through generations, and affect your life in very unique ways, you are ready to assess your own current patterns. You have balanced your emotional state. Next, you need absolute peace and calmness of mind.

This Mudra will help you achieve that state, so you can begin understanding and also finding solutions with clarity and focus. Only you can accomplish this, as it is only you that knows all the inner makings of your most hidden fears, hesitations, or other concealed automatic responses you have to various situations, dynamics, people, environmental elements or topics.

Practice this Mudra to find an absolutely balanced state of your mind and become a detail oriented detective, exploring your own inner makings. This is great intrinsic work that is required in order to transform and overcome PTSD of any kind.

CHAKRAS
All Chakras

HEALING COLORS
All Colors

AFFIRMATION

MY MIND IS IN PERFECT BALANCE AND HARMONY

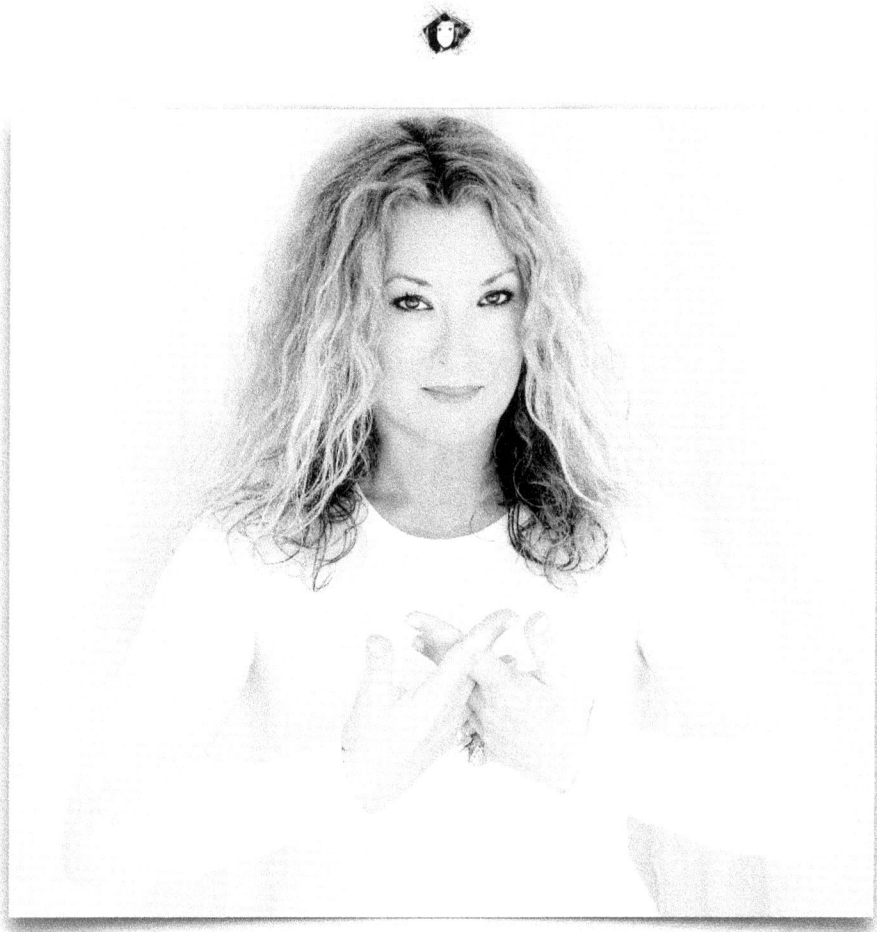

Sit with a straight back, shoulders down, nice and relaxed. Bend your elbows, lift the hands up in front of your solar plexus or chest area and interlace the fingers backward with palms facing up. Fingers are pointing up and are straight. Concentrate on the tension in your fingers and magnified energy in your hands spreading throughout your body and creating a balanced mindset. Practice for Three minutes.

BREATH
LONG, DEEP AND SLOW THRU YOUR NOSE

MANTRA
GOBINDAY, MUKUNDAY, UDARAAY, APAARAY,
HARYING, KARYNG, NIRNAMAY, AKAMAY
(Sustainer, Liberator, Enlightener, Infinite, Destroyer, Creator, Nameless, Desire-less)

Week Four

THE PROCESS OF RELEASE

Y ou are now well on your way through this deeply intense, soul-searching, healing, and empowering process. Hopefully you've identified and recognized the nature of your past wounds, as well as intricate PTSD patterns that hold a grip on your subconscious mind, and prevent you from moving forward into your optimal life. This is the turning point. You are now ready to release your past and every painful, unwanted emotion connected to your PTSD that may carry undesirable associations.

IT IS SIMPLY THE LAW OF PHYSICS THAT YOU CANNOT WELCOME THE NEW, UNLESS AND UNTIL YOU RELEASE THE OLD.

You've arrived at the conscious conclusion and realization that you just don't have the extra space to "house" anything that is not in your best interest. Now it's time to change your inner world. There is a deeply healing aspect to the act of release. From the subtle energy perspective, you are liberating yourself from the invisible energy cords, strings, and obstructing bonds that keep you entangled and connected to something that may seem time-wise and physically far away, yet on subtle realms, it is still very much alive. Time and distance do not weaken these cords. They may be buried deep in your psyche, but nevertheless, they are still there. Until now, you've kept them hidden, out of sight, but now you've looked at them bravely, examined and faced them. The moment of release is here. Now let's find out how this process applies to your unique situation. When something you'll read rings a bell, and sounds similar to your own situation, you will intuitively know you're on the right track.

PTSD, ENERGY CORDS AND ATTACHMENTS

The energy cords of attachments are much talked about, and therefore it is truly essential that you understand their complex nature, and what they represent. Once you'll understand the basics, you can proceed through the process of releasing unwanted cords and freeing your energy body.

I want to clarify the specifics of energy cords that we are speaking about, because most often if not always, energy cords are assumed to be only between romantic relationship partners. But keep in mind, that energy cords are present in all interactions that contain emotional involvement. They are not present only in love relationships, although this is how we most often describe and understand them.

THE ENERGY CORDS CAN KEEP YOU CONNECTED TO ANOTHER PERSON WITH WHOM YOU ARE SHARING ANY KIND OF EMOTIONAL DYNAMIC.

Energy cords can also link you to a particular situation or geographical location, but most often it will always be another person that plays a role in past trauma, who is somehow connected with, or represents the negative side of your past experience.

Let's say you were lost on a deserted island, but the person who traveled with you there, or found you and rescued you is involved, even if indirectly. Your PTSD includes them, and their presence can trigger a PTSD experience. And obviously, if someone harmed you in any way, you have an energy cord with them as well. It won't be a cord that ever contained emotions of love, but rather the opposite. Still, it is a subtle energy cord. Your continued dislike of that person, sustains the cord. If the cord is with a person who was once your partner, the wound is deeper and the cord is stronger. Why? Because at one time, you opened your heart and allowed them full access to your energy core.

REMOVING PTSD ENERGY CORDS

We often hear of healing practitioners that are engaged in "cutting cords" for their clients. There are many people who do not want to work on their own inner makings or unhealthy states, and just want a quick remedy.

For example: if you suffer from headaches, you may just want to reach for that aspirin or pain killer and forget all about it. Examining the source of your headache would require some work and soul searching. So you prefer to take the fast instant-cure option. But the truth is, you cannot heal, if you refuse to look into the depths of your very own being. Therefore, a painkiller is just a short-term solution.

Similarly, with subtle energy complex dynamics like energy cords of attachments, that keep us in a state of unpleasant, suffering standstill — we usually want a quick and painless solution.

What to do? Why not call someone who can relieve you of your "pain"? I know of so many cases where gifted energy workers are often burdened with impatient and ignorant requests from their clients: "I need you to cut my cord with this person!" And often the energy worker embarks on this useless process, helping cleanse someone's auric field and temporarily weaken the disruptive energy cord. But keep in mind – such an endeavor can be accomplished only by a truly well heeled healing practitioner, and even if they accomplish the task, it will be a very temporarily solution. So it is really a pointless and thankless effort.

The client may feel relief for a little while, a few hours or perhaps days, while there is no guarantee, that this could even be accomplished. But what is guaranteed, is the fact that the old "problem" and energy cord will reemerge and stubbornly reestablish its persistent, strong presence. What happens next, is that the client becomes even more disappointed, forlorn and lost. They assume that since the healer could not help them, no-one and nobody can. So looking from a long-term perspective, it is not advisable to offer these kinds of services in the first place.

Why? Because it will backfire and throw the person even deeper into their victim and helpless pattern.

THE TRUTH IS, WE ARE REQUIRED TO CONSCIOUSLY PARTICIPATE AND MAKE AN EFFORT TO HELP OURSELVES.

And this is rarely an easy process. Keep in mind, we all have certain emotional energy cords with others. So even if you find an energy worker that could attempt to cut your invisible energy cords that connect you to an unpleasant event, or another person that is affecting you in a negative or painful way, it simply is not as easy to eliminate, as people may imagine.

It is almost as absurd as expecting that someone else will breathe instead of you – they simply can't. You have to breathe on your own, and similarly, only you can dismantle your cords – on your own. These invisible cords are a living and breathing part of you. They are sustained by your feelings, emotional states, mental energy-thoughts, and attachments.

> **UNTIL YOU CONTINUE TO DWELL ON THE TRIGGER - PERSON,**
> **OR ARE AFFECTED BY UNRESOLVED ISSUES,**
> **THE ENERGY CORD EXISTS AND INHIBITS YOUR SUBTLE BODY.**

This kind of congested state prevents a healthy and natural flow of energy. As a consequence, your physical body, mental disposition, and emotional state, are all affected and limited in function. Once you truly understand how powerful the energy of your thoughts is, how magnetic the energy of your emotions is, and how authoritative the energy of your patterns is, you become awake and aware. You are prepared to consciously make an effort and shift your focus, your intention, your feelings, attachments and grudges, that have kept you captive.

Opening and preparing for this shift of consciousness is deeply transformative, since it unburdens your very core and unleashes energy that was imprisoned, often for a very long time. Just imagine these examples: if you've been harboring unresolved feelings towards a past love relationship partner, your energy field is busy sustaining this cord of resentment, hurt and anger. This results in your inability to have space for a new, healthier, and happier relationship. You may say you are still "hung up" on the past partner, but in esoteric terms, you are unknowingly sustaining the invisible cord of connection with them, even if it's a bad one. This can go on for a very long time.

Similar dynamic of energy cord, can be maintained with any person that emotionally affected you – perhaps a boss that fired you, an attacker that abused you, a stranger that violated you, or a dear friend that betrayed you. If you still harbor unresolved feelings towards them or suffer from PTSD connected to that relationship, you are sustaining the cord.

SENSING A PULL ON YOUR SUBTLE ENERGY CORDS

I wish to clarify something very important here: if you are of sensitive nature and naturally very receptive – which a lot of healing practitioners are – the energy cords can work in numerous complex ways. You may feel resolved about a past enemy, but somehow still feel some kind of inexplicable occasional wave of friction between you two, even if you never see or speak to each other.

You are convinced that you are resolved and forgave them and have let them go, but the fact that you feel these waves of negativity, feels very confusing to you. And rightfully so. The truth is, you may be simply picking up the negativity emitting from them. You are sensing their negative attachment to you, which of course results in disturbing effect on you.

YOU MAY FEEL THE UNPLEASANT FREQUENCY OF SOMEONE THAT HAS ENERGY ACCESS TO YOU THROUGH THE INVISIBLE CORD.

You will feel this ONLY IF your are vulnerable, or very sensory alert, otherwise you may not feel anything at all. This is complicated but quite common. It is very important that you are clear and honest with yourself in assessing if you really still harbor negative feelings towards someone, or a challenging situation they were involved with, or pain they may have caused you. If you have let it go, but still feel occasional waves of negativity in connection with them, you are simply sensing their disposition, and are strong enough to consciously eliminate the cord and prevent it from re-establishing. You have the upper hand because you recognize the dynamic. You may wonder why the cord is still alive after all this time?

HOW DOES A CORD GET ESTABLISHED?

A cord can only be created, if and when you open up and allow another person to energetically attach themselves to you. A cord cannot be established by simply walking around and having a preying person invade your energy space. It can only happen, if you are vulnerable, open and accessible.

WHAT MAKES YOU ENERGETICALLY ACCESSIBLE?

A few different situations and states can be the cause of your vulnerable and easy accessibility. It could be your own weakened, fearful or depleted energy state, lack of self-confidence, or a desperate search for someone to rescue you. In other words, you are looking for someone to give you the power that you alone do not have.

Another situation that makes you extremely vulnerable, is the use of any and all mind-altering drugs, that considerably weaken your auric shield. You become open to draining negative and addictive cords from others that are in similar energy-weakened and polluted states. If you have an addiction, your auric shield is easily permeable, this makes you very vulnerable to invasive energy cords, especially with other addicts who are similarly weak and need other people's energy to sustain them.

An example would be an addict who relapses when in bad company or a depleted state. They cannot sustain the resistance to invasive cords, and are easily overpowered. And of course, opening your heart to someone else, makes you very vulnerable and extremely accessible for them to enter your energy field, and attach themselves to your energy core.

> **THROUGH A PHYSICAL INTERCOURSE, YOUR PARTNER'S AURIC FIELD MERGES WITH YOURS AND INSTANTLY ESTABLISHES A CORD.**

Now you become easily accessible, will quickly affect and influence each other, and are deeply energetically connected. This is not necessarily bad, and in love relationships and friendships it is almost inevitable, however, if and when a relationship turns negative, this presents a great and long-term danger. A cord can also happen in any kind of imbalanced parasitical interaction, when you give more than you receive in return, and have others hanging on you, and persistently draining your energy.

VAMPIRIC PTSD ENERGY CORDS

Now we arrive at the much-talked-about topic of people that drain our energy. Anyone who drains your energy is an energy vampire. Such a person functions in a parasitical energy pattern, and is unable to sustain their own level of energy. They continuously prey on others to survive.

How is this connected to PTSD? Attaching to others to supplement their own depleted energy states is connected to the person's own wounds and patterns. And keep in mind – you are perhaps also an energy drain on others, especially if you cannot sustain your own energy field. That may not be fun to hear, but it is possible.

What would indicate this? If you have an addiction to perpetual drama, require non-stop attention, need others to solve your problems, are in a persistent victim pattern, unable to make your own decisions, or can't live without someone boosting up your ego – all these states indicate that you need others to function. You may need others in many different ways and whatever it is, your energy state has a codependent nature and you are unable or simply unwilling to function on your own. What is important for us to know especially in regard to PTSD, is that a wound from the past makes you vulnerable in whatever area your wound resides. And it makes you vulnerable to become an energy draining person yourself. And that is not pleasant. Because somewhere deep inside you are very aware of your imbalance or lack of independence.

Do not confuse this with natural healthy relationship dynamics. In all relationships there is a certain level of interdependence, that is one of marvels of a great relationship – that you are hopefully an equal team. But here we are talking about a different kind of dynamic, where you actually burden the other person with your own discontent and continuously demand too much. Or they demand too much of you. The energy cord becomes an indicator of an imbalanced draining dynamic between two people.

Usually that is not much talked about, because everyone always wants to know how to get rid of an energy vampire, without ever even thinking of a possibility, that they themselves could be that energy vampire. Or perhaps they are facilitating the dysfunctional dynamic.

But here we do have to address this dynamic as well, because through the process of healing, we have to take into consideration all possible aspects. And PTSD is tightly connected with this synergy.

IF YOU ARE SURROUNDED BY ENERGY VAMPIRES, YOU HAVE TO TAKE RESPONSIBILITY FOR YOUR PART. YOU HAVE ALLOWED THEM TO ATTACH AND SUSTAIN THEMSELVES THROUGH THE ENERGY CORDS.

An example would be when you have everyone depend on you, and complain about it, but in truth you are a control freak and like that you control everything. Energy cords help you supervise the entire interaction. Another example would be, if someone's survival depends on you and you encourage them to remain in this vulnerable state, in order to control them. They are energetically attached to you while you sustain them, and yet you complain about it. You are definitely a part of this problematic energy cord connection.

Similarly in a relationship where a partner is draining and possessive and you give them a reason to remain that way, while behaving a certain way. Perhaps you are betraying them, not being truthful with them, or playing with their emotions, in order to manipulate them. You have a cord with them and yet they live in constant fear of being betrayed, abandoned or hurt. Your behavior helps sustain this dynamic. You feed off their engaged energy.

How is this connected to PTSD? If in the past or even in their childhood, a person was mistreated by their parents who made their love and attention conditional or showed sibling preferences, this is a PTSD pattern that has followed them into later adult life, and relationship behavior.

But wait! We were talking about energy pattern in previous chapter, so is this the same thing? No, this is about the PTSD effects on subtle energy fields, creating cords, and how they carry over into your PRESENT LIFE, unless you release them. Is this only a matter of a repeated patterns? It is in fact a bit more complicated than that.

The wound of the past establishes an energy cord that remains with you into today. If you don't heal and remove it, the cord lives on and affects every aspect of your life. You see, if you have an energy cord codependence or unhealthy relationship in whatever way, this becomes the new normal. If the person who was previously energetically attached leaves your life, OR for example, you leave a home where you were abused, OR you leave a town or a job or a relationship where the trauma occurred, you may be able to detach and remove that cord. Changing environments often helps. BUT, here lies often the problem:

WHEREVER THE CORD WAS, YOU NOW HAVE A WOUND, THAT LEAVES A VOID — OPEN AND ACCESSIBLE TO A NEW, SIMILAR, OR EVEN IDENTICAL CORD ATTACHMENT.

This is why very often, immediately after one dysfunctional relationship ends, a person gets into another relationship where a very similar, almost identical dynamic repeats itself. The PTSD depleted state, with an ethereal wound, makes us vulnerable to immediately replace the energy cord with another one, to prevent an energy tear from completely leaking our energy. One can say, well, the person has bad luck, when in fact all they've done is simply patched up the previous wound with a replacement that energetically matches with that wound. This creates an ongoing PTSD challenge that follows one through life, unless they consciously step out of it.

ACCOUNTABILITY

Let's be clear, it is impossible to heal an old trauma if you don't take some level of personal responsibility for whatever situation occurred.

**IF YOU WERE IN AN ABUSIVE RELATIONSHIP
AND ALLOWED IT TO CONTINUE,
IT WILL BE LIBERATING AND HEALING TO REALIZE AND ADMIT,
THAT TO A CERTAIN POINT, YOU ALLOWED IT TO BE SO.**

Why? Because this way you begin to weaken the emotional bond with the other person. You are taking your power back, and abandoning the state of victimhood. Yes, you fell prey to a difficult situation, but you played a certain role. Perhaps it was the same role you grew up with, while witnessing your parents, but to a certain degree the role was familiar and bearable to you. You might have even considered it normal. Once you realize that there is nothing normal about an abusive relationship, you open up the possibility to leave. Even if it takes you a little while to make that happen, once your heart ceases to succumb to persuasion that love equals pain, you are out, one step closer to freedom.

This of course does not apply to all trauma. If you were a victim of an attack, a violent assault, or any other very aggressive traumatic experience of that nature, you are in no way to blame.

**IF TRAUMA HAPPENED TO YOU BECAUSE YOU WERE SIMPLY
IN A WRONG PLACE AT THE WRONG TIME,
OR WERE NAIVE, DIDN'T HAVE THE KNOWLEDGE,
EXPERIENCE OR STRENGTH TO AVOID IT,
YOU ARE NOT TO BLAME IN ANY WAY.**

But if your trauma was of a different nature, where you were actually given a few choices, but stayed in a dangerous situation on purpose, perhaps from stubbornness, or in the heat of an argument, or because you loved someone despite the fact that they abused you, in such a case, you do have to take partial responsibility. This will help you detach the energy cord, and abolish the belief of helplessness.

PTSD AND CHAKRA CORD CONNECTIONS

In case of severe trauma where your choice did not play any kind of a factor, your energy cord detachment process will have to be through healing steps in Chakra scale order. This will be the path to regaining balance and strength. Here are some examples of trauma and how your energy body is involved:

1. In case of SEXUAL ABUSE OR ASSAULT, this creates acute PTSD in areas of 1, 2, and 3 Chakra. As a consequence, the 4, 5, 6, 7 will be substantially weakened.

2. In case of PHYSICAL ABUSE OR ASSAULT, this creates acute PTSD mostly in areas of 1. and 3. Chakra.

3. In case of EMOTIONAL ABUSE OR PSYCHOLOGICAL MISTREATMENT, this creates acute PTSD in areas of 3, 4, 5, 6, and 7 Chakra.

4. In case of NEGLECT, this creates acute PTSD in areas of 1, 3, 4 Chakra.

5. In case of SERIOUS ACCIDENT, ILLNESS, OR MEDICAL PROCEDURE, this creates acute PTSD in Chakra 1, as well as all other Chakras

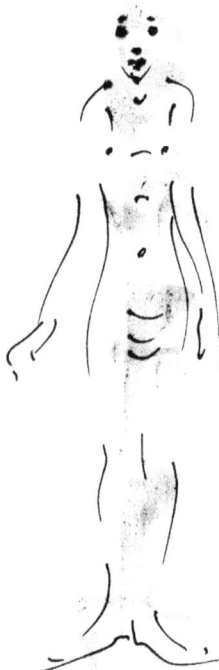

6. In case of HISTORICAL TRAUMA this creates PTSD in all Chakras.

7. In case of VICTIM OR WITNESS TO DOMESTIC VIOLENCE, this creates acute PTSD in Chakras 1, 3, 4.

8. In case of VICTIM OR WITNESS TO COMMUNITY VIOLENCE, this creates acute PTSD in all Chakras.

If the child is UNDER THE AGE OF 9, the trauma will be most acute and long - term in relation to their age.

If they are 4 YEARS OLD, their fourth chakra will receive most damage.

If they are 5 YEARS OLD, their fifth chakra will be affected, and so on. These are the years that correspond to the process of establishing a more dense energy state in each chakra. A child age 5, will be differently affected by divorce than a child at age 3. The five year old will suffer in area of communication, expression, and telling the truth – all fifth Chakra matters. A child age 3, under stress of divorce, will demonstrate outburst of anger, fear and ego imbalance.

It's important to mention that older people are usually in a state of weakened physical energy level, and therefore have a tendency to need other people's subtle energy. This kind of dynamic can happen with their children who are emotionally accessible to them, and easily connected by the subtle energy cord. This is a very difficult topic as family cord interaction is a natural dynamic, however, a depleted and parasitical energy connection is not healthy.

How to overcome this challenge? Awareness and resistance to unending energy attachment must be established.

YOUR PARTICIPATION IN TRAUMA

Another important question remains: Were you a willing and engaged participant in your trauma?

For example, a war veteran suffering from PTSD will experience a very different manifestation of symptoms than a victim of a natural disaster. A war veteran consciously chose to engage in profession that holds a very high potential for traumatic experiences. He is somewhat prepared and trained to expect the worst. It doesn't make his PTSD any easier, quite to the contrary, and certainly remains very uniquely challenging.

A regular citizen who happens to live through a fire, earthquake or any other natural disaster, feels utterly helpless and victimized in a very different way. A war veteran has time to prepare, a victim of earthquake has less of an opportunity for that. A very important question remains: why would anyone consciously select to expose themselves to trauma?
A tremendous desire to protect others and serve their country – this is noble and understandable. Especially so, if other family members in generations before them chose the same calling.

A SENSE OF DUTY TO PROTECT OR HELP OTHERS IS A NOBLE REASON AND CAUSE TO CONSCIOUSLY PARTICIPATE IN TRAUMATIC EVENTS, SUCH AS WAR OR RESCUE MISSIONS.

But why would anyone choose to enter and remain in an abusive relationship? Most likely caused by previous patterns of dysfunctional parents and traumatic childhood. The person simply expects relationships to be violent, abusive, and filled with conflict. If one was raised with painful experiences related to their parents, they will be inclined to gravitate towards similar partners. In their distorted perception, love equals pain, punishment, disrespect, abandonment and conflict.

> **FROM ESOTERIC PERSPECTIVE, IF YOU HAVE AURA WOUNDS WITH COMPLEX ENERGY CORDS, ONCE YOU REMOVE THEM, YOU WILL BE INCLINED TO PATCH THEM UP WITH SIMILAR CORDS.**

War veterans can benefit and strengthen their resilience when overcoming PTSD, by addressing all chakra energy centers and reviewing their childhood pre-set patterns, and individual disposition that played a role in selecting their calling and career choice. Understanding the deeper aspects of their emotional dispositions, mental attitude, and inherited soul energy, will help them gain control over the trauma they endured, and see it from a position of strength and supreme resilience, and not helpless victimhood. A hero who claims his wounds is empowered and at peace. A soldier who relates to his experiences as a victim, needs to reclaim his power of choices he made, and conquer the darkness he witnessed, by holding the indestructible inner Light of resilience and strength. Once he relates to past trauma from position of fortitude, his healing process begins.

RELEASE AND REPLACE

In order to heal and disable the cord, a release is needed, followed by immediate healthy replacement with positive energy. The most effective way to remove the cord is by recognition. Once you identify it, it immediately loses energy and becomes weaker.

Let's say you are traumatized in Chakra I. area of survival and security. When you recognize this weakness and trauma in your energy system, you can release it and immediately replace it with a positive counter effective energy. Allowing for an emotional release is extremely powerful. Recognizing the negative mental patterns and speaking or writing about them, begins the process of letting go. At the core of past pain and trauma lies fear that expresses itself in grief, anxiety, nervousness, paranoia and insecurity. Intentionally releasing all negativity and continuously affirming your resolve and determination, will help you overcome the past and weaken the cord of attachment that suffocated your subtle body.

THE USUAL CORD ATTACHMENT AREAS

The most common cord areas of attachment are the 1, 2, 3 and 4th chakra. Why? Because the higher chakras do not tie you to earthly attachments, but lift you into higher realms. The Chakra 1. cord is obviously connected to sheer survival. If you depend on someone else for your survival, you have a cord with them in that area. Or they may depend on you for their safety and survival, like for example; a small child. You are vulnerable in this area and may tolerate some kind of trauma simply, because otherwise you have no means of surviving.

How to harmonize this? In order to avoid PTSD energy cords in CHAKRA 1, make an effort to gain independence, and consciously try to gain balance. Even small steps will help you overcome negative aspects and promote the positive ones. In CHAKRA 2. the cord connection is related to creative and sexual energy. If you have a negative cord in that area, consciously see and realize this unhealthy dynamic, and begin the challenging process of detaching. You will succeed when you begin to understand what aspects of this cord are unhealthy for you, and recognize why you tolerate them. If your cord connection is in CHAKRA 3, it has to do with ego, control, mind matters, fear and anger. It is a power center. If you have a cord with someone who controls or overpowers you, it requires healing. The CHAKRA 4. cord is obviously connected to matters of the heart and love. However, this cord can also be challenging when in negative manifestation such as betrayal, emotional distance, no response to one's love, and inability to express emotions. If this is the cord you are encountering, you can heal and balance it by recognizing true feelings in your heart, and how your past affected the present. Whatever the challenge of your cord connection with another person, you will immediately improve, simply by clearly recognizing the unhealthy dynamic. This is the key step in the healing process. And if you are sustaining any kind of negative cords, they will prevent you from releasing the past PTSD elements. The key now for you is to examine if you have any past negative emotional cords that are still binding you to someone or something else. This is the last step required to free your energy field.

ANY STRONG EMOTION THAT TIES YOU TO SOMEONE OR AN EVENT, IS A SIGN THAT AN ENERGY CORD STILL EXISTS.

Release begins with your awareness, recognition and understanding of all elements that played a role and contributed to your trauma. Now you are ready for the next step of actively cleansing and empowering your subtle energy field.

YOUR ASSIGNMENT

AFFIRMATION

> ## I SEE ALL MY ENERGY CORDS AND CHOOSE TO KEEP ONLY THE ONES OF RETURNED LOVE

DIARY

In this chapter your are recognizing and analyzing any and all energy cords from the past that are still alive – here in the present. The moment you'll recognize them, they will weaken. If you feel cords with someone else that you thought were resolved, examine if they are originating with the other person and not with you. If that is so, you will be able to detach them quickly and efficiently. Claim your power and be in charge of your auric shield.

No one that you do not consciously choose and allow, can attach themselves to you.

PROCESS

Work thru the questions, come back in a few days, see if anything changed, add it on, clarify and self-discover through the process.

PRACTICE

This week is about observing your auric shield and sensing any cords that drain your energy field. Old cords associated with your past trauma are ready to be released. Make space for all new and harmonious energy that will sustain your auric shield, and resiliently defend you against unwanted energy cords. Review, reflect, analyze and repeat. You will find all causes and understand your deepest self-imposed restrictions. The moment you accomplish this, freedom is within reach. You will be amazed at what you'll discover and uncover in the deepest corners of your past. This is your energy field, and you are in charge. Demonstrate this by consciously seeing beyond the usual. See beyond – see within.

> ### YOUR AURIC SHIELD IS SACRED. PROTECT IT.
> ### CAREFULLY DISCERN WHOM YOU ALLOW TO TOUCH IT,
> ### OR ENTER INTO YOUR ORBIT.

RECOGNIZE YOUR ENERGY CORDS

1. DO YOU HAVE OLD ENERGY CORDS THAT HOLD YOU IN THE PAST?

2. DO YOU HAVE ANY CURRENT NEGATIVE ENERGY CORDS WITH ANOTHER PERSON?

3. DO YOU FEEL ENERGY CORDS OF ANGER? FROM WHOM?

4. DO YOU FEEL ENERGY CORDS OF FEAR? WITH WHOM?

5. DO YOU FEEL DRAINING ENERGY CORDS? WITH WHOM?

6. DO YOU FEEL ENERGY CORDS OF UNFULFILLED LOVE ? WITH WHOM?

7. ARE YOU READY TO LET GO OF CORDS YOU DON'T NEED AND BECOME FREE?

MUDRAS as ENERGY EQUALIZERS

Mudras are ideal and most powerful formula for old trauma release. Why?

Because the intricate hand and finger positions open up your nadis – energy channels, and Chakras, and help them cleanse, recharge, and re-establish a self-sustaining, powerful, vibrant, and healthy energy field. An overall empowered auric state diminishes the overwhelming drain and hold of energy cords, and helps maintain a balance.

In a way, Mudras are like energy equalizers that harmonize the fine balance between all your energy centers and countless energy cords. This way, even if you have a persistent PTSD energy cord that connects you to a person or past trauma, the healthy chakras and active nadis will help heal, balance and remove any disproportionate subtle energy shortcomings or burdening congestions. This will help you regain your power. You will not continue sustaining anyone else with any kind of emotional attachment, and will eliminate access to you, and your energy source.

With Mudra practice your own energy field becomes optimally charged, and the negative cords cease to overpower your entire being. If the cords are negative in nature, they will weaken, and eventually completely dissipate and disappear. The healing and removal of negative cords occurs naturally, when you strengthen your own energy body on your own.

MUDRA of DIVINE WORSHIP

Sit with a straight back and keep your shoulders down, nice and relaxed. Join the palms of your hands in front of your chest. Sit still and concentrate on your Third Eye for at least Three minutes.

BREATH
LONG, DEEP AND SLOW THRU YOUR NOSE

MANTRA
EK ONG KAR
(One Creator, God Is One)

CHAKRAS
ALL CHAKRAS

HEALING COLORS
ALL COLORS

AFFIRMATION

I AM ONE WITH DIVINE FORCE, I AM PEACE

MUDRA FOR OVERCOMING ANXIETY

Sit with a straight back and keep your shoulders down, nice and relaxed. Bend your elbows and raise your arms so your upper arms are parallel to the ground and extended out to the sides. Your fingers are spread wide and pointing up to the sky. Start rotating your hands back and forth, pivoting at the wrists. You will go thru a period that seems difficult, but remain persistent and it will become easier. Practice for Three minutes, then relax, and enjoy the sensations.

BREATH
LONG, DEEP AND SLOW THRU YOUR NOSE

MANTRA
HARKANAM SAT NAM

(God's Name Is Truth)

CHAKRAS
HEART - 4, THROAT - 5, THIRD EYE - 6

HEALING COLORS
GREEN, BLUE, INDIGO

AFFIRMATION

I RELEASE ALL ANXIETY AND REPLACE IT WITH PEACE

MUDRA FOR HELP WITH A GRAVE SITUATION

Sit with a straight back and keep your shoulders down, nice and relaxed. Bend your elbows and place both palms on your upper chest, fingers together and pointing toward each other. Feel the healing energy of your hands soothing your heart. Hold for Three minutes, then relax.

BREATH

LONG, DEEP AND SLOW THRU YOUR NOSE

MANTRA

HUMME HUM, BRAHAM HUM, BRAHAM HUM

(Calling upon Your Infinite Self)

CHAKRA

HEART - 4

HEALING COLOR

GREEN

AFFIRMATION

I SOOTHE MY BODY, MIND, HEART AND SOUL

MUDRA FOR FACING FEAR

Sit with a straight back, shoulders down, nice and relaxed. Bend your right elbow and lift the arm up to level of your face. Face your palm outward, fingers together as if taking a vow. Hold your left hand in front of your navel, palm facing up, fingers together. Concentrate on energy flowing into your hands, practice for Three minutes.

BREATH
LONG, DEEP AND SLOW THRU YOUR NOSE

MANTRA
NIRBHAO NIRVAIR AKAAL MORT

(Fearless, Without Enemy, Immortal Personified God)

CHAKRAS
SOLAR PLEXUS - 3, CROWN - 7

HEALING COLORS
YELLOW, VIOLET

AFFIRMATION

I AM FEARLESS, I AM BRAVE

MUDRA FOR RELEASING NEGATIVE EMOTIONS

Sit with a straight back and keep your shoulders down, nice and relaxed. Make fists with both hands, bend your arms and bring them up in front of your heart. Cross your left arm over right while keeping your fists turned outwards. Hold for Three minutes then relax.

BREATH

LONG, DEEP AND SLOW THRU YOUR NOSE

MANTRA

OMM

(God in His Absolute State)

CHAKRA

HEART - 4

HEALING COLOR

GREEN

AFFIRMATION

I RELEASE AND LET GO, I AM FREE AND CLEAR. I AM LIGHT.

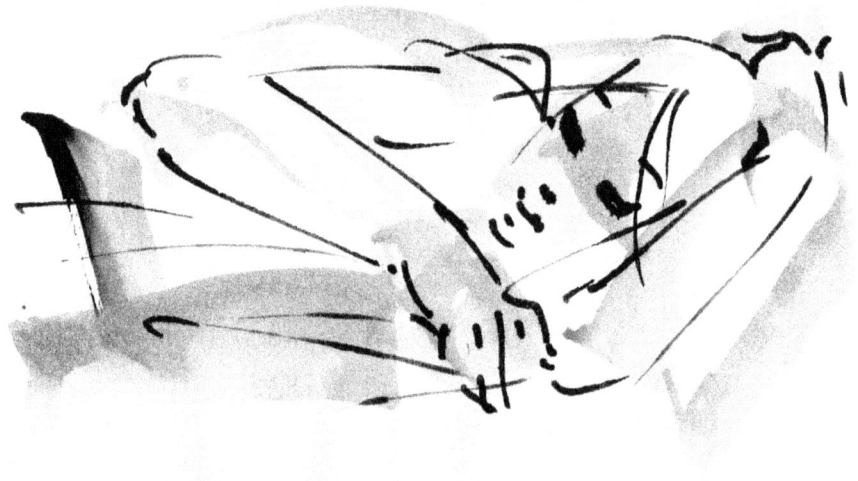

Week Five

YOUR HEALING SPACE

Y ou are now ready to commence the next vital step in your healing process. To achieve a full recovery from PTSD, you need to have certain mechanisms in place in order to provide optimal circumstances for a most positive outcome.

There is one non-negotiable circumstance that has to be assured in order for you to be able to heal on any level, and that is **your environment**. A very wise and extraordinary yoga Master Paramahansa Yogananda said: *"Environment is stronger than your will."* And this is true.

NO MATTER HOW STRONG YOU WILLPOWER IS, IF YOU ARE IN A NEGATIVE, DRAINING, OR DISRUPTIVE ENVIRONMENT, YOUR HEALING PROCESS IS GOING TO BE THWARTED.

Your environment does not entail just to your livings pace, but actually every environmental element that you encounter during the day, and could influence or affect you in a negative or traumatic way. Just think about it: if your PTSD is connected to assault and you still have somehow indirect contact with the assailant, or occasionally encounter them near your home, it is beyond challenging to assume you will be able to heal. You may be resilient and manage to protect yourself from continuous attacks, but your PTSD is going to continue on – in a different manifestation. It will require incredible strength to stand your ground, remain defiant and strong. Any kind of trauma related circumstance in your immediate home or work everyday-environment is simply draining and unhealthy.

Until you are free from that dynamic, your "environment" remains toxic. Any aspects of disruptive environment that block your successful healing process may downright prevent you from overcoming a certain traumatic situation. In this chapter we will look at the many environmental elements that need to be remedied, before you can expect to accelerate your healing.

WHATEVER YOUR PTSD EMOTIONAL REACTIVE BEHAVIOR IS, IT WILL BE DIFFICULT TO ELIMINATE, UNTIL YOUR ENVIRONMENT IS HEALTHY.

For example: if your PTSD reactive state is to find comfort in food, and you are surrounded with people that exhibit very unhealthy eating habits, you cannot expect to be able to sustain a healthy diet, while everyone around you indulges in unhealthy behavior – this will simply provoke your reactive negative habit. Similarly, this dynamic will reappear if one is struggling with addiction to drugs, alcohol or any other habit-forming tendencies. Your environment has so many complex circumstances that may affect you and play a decisive role in how you handle and overcome PTSD triggered activities or behavior, that may not be in your best interest.

We will look at various categories that play an important role to help you observe, notice, and decide, which areas of your daily environment are helping and supporting your healthy efforts, and which continue to keep you trapped in a traumatized, yet perhaps familiar and negative behavior patterns.

It is up to you to make decisions in regard to your own life, and once you will clearly see the big picture, your inner awareness will not let you rest until you remedy the disturbing elements. You can accomplish what you set out to do. Hopefully, your clear desire to create and overall harmonious, supportive, healthy and loving environment for yourself will prevail and you will succeed.

This may be one of your life's greatest challenges, but once you gain control of it, you will open up the field of endless possibilities to experience, accomplish, and contribute to this world whatever your heart desires. We are cleaning house, clearing old unwanted debris, and creating an open space for healing, happiness, health and love.

YOUR HOME

Your living space is where you sleep, wake up, enjoy company of family, loved ones and close friends. It is where you prepare your food and find a safe space for rejuvenation, relaxation and rest. No matter how luxurious or spartan, the one element that cannot be ignored, is safety and comfort.

Do you feel safe in your own home? Are you comfortable to let go, and truly deeply restore and strengthen yourself, so you can properly function and face challenges? This may seem completely logical and obvious to some – the ones who are fortunate to have this luxury. To others, who suffer from disturbances in their intimate home environment, this is a very challenging topic. If one of your co-habitants is the cause of your PTSD, it is pretty obvious you will not be able to recover or establish a healthy pattern. If your home is not safe, has difficult living partners, or perhaps an ignorant neighbor's noise pollution, or any other disturbing element that also contributes to your stress, you need to pay attention and recognize this. If your home is shared with someone who leads a very unhealthy lifestyle, this will affect you in negative ways. You need your basic healthy lifestyle needs covered in order to heal. Very often, it is impossible to simply abandon your home and leave the trigger of PTSD behind. Various circumstances, family duties, partnerships, or children, may force you to stay in a challenging situation, that continuously adds to your unhealthy state and accelerates the PTSD effects. Even if that is the case, there is a first step that will help you in your healing process, and that is awareness.

WHEN YOU RECOGNIZE THE UNHEALTHY ASPECTS YOU ARE ENDURING IN YOUR HOME ARE NOT SOMETHING YOU SHOULD TOLERATE, YOU CAN BEGIN THE PROCESS OF "LIBERATION."

If an oppressive person that lives in your immediate environment is contributing to your traumatized state, you need to clearly recognize it, so you can begin to systematically establish a certain zone of safety. Ideal solution would be to leave this negative situation, but since nothing in life is easy or ideal, this may not be possible. However, your awareness will help you gain strength, so that you can begin finding and establishing a physical location or area, where you have total privacy and peace. Perhaps you can establish one specific room for yourself, where you can be undisturbed and peaceful. This will help you gain strength so that you can eventually completely liberate yourself from the oppressive situation, or at least re-establish new rules where you are not continuously suffering.

A DOSE OF REALITY

It is quite often the case, that the person suffering from PTSD is unfortunately still living in circumstances that caused it. This may not have to do anything with another person, but rather a challenging circumstance.

For example, if you are challenged financially and are always fearing for your survival, your situation will always sustain your ongoing PTSD, even if you live in harmony with co-habitants. The aspect of financial struggle will envelop your home situation.

In such a case your home is an intricate part of your PTSD, so you can't simply snap your fingers and move to a better situation – you have to learn to manage it better, so that it allows you the basic possibility to function as healthy as possible, despite the challenging existential circumstances. So many people struggle financially, which causes them ongoing PTSD in regard to this existential fear. What they can do, is change their disposition and understanding of a financial struggle, so that they continue to search for solutions, implement financial restructure and eventually overcome this challenge. PTSD may still follow them for quite a while, but with time, the longer they live in a stable environment, the faster their PTSD will heal, and with time and they will overcome it.

Another example would be if you live with a partner or family member that is causing you PTSD with an ongoing traumatic disposition – again, you may not be able to immediately remove yourself from the ongoing toxic dynamic, BUT you can learn to manage it better, so that you maintain a sense of peace, despite the challenge. This requires strength and confidence, that your life can and will improve. You need to begin building a plan for a better future. If this entails leaving your home, then so be it. These are challenging situations, but they can be overcome. Obviously, our life circumstances are rarely simple, but are extremely complex, sometimes long-term, and often very draining and limiting to us.

Learning how to recognize and function despite the challenges is the key. This demands for exploring various possibilities, of how to find the best solution, but they all involve your own healthy dose of courage, confidence, self-respect and sense of self-worth. If someone or a circumstance is continuously challenging your self-confidence, you must gather all your strength and consciously make an effort to shift the challenging dynamics.

> **WHENEVER YOU MAKE AN EFFORT, THE UNIVERSE WILL ALWAYS EVENTUALLY HELP YOU. IT SIMPLY HAS TO.**

Sitting passively and giving up will not bring the desired results, in fact it is going to sink you deeper into your challenge. A fighting spirit, a patient but persistent effort, and an ability to find positive elements no matter how dire your situation… all of those principles will help you manage a challenging environmental situation. Of course the challenge may not be solely at home, it could be at work or somewhere in a society, where you are outcast for whatever reason. This remains your immediate environment and unless you can leave and relocate, you will have to find a way to reemerge, and create a safe and healing space, no matter the challenge. We are talking about endless variety of PTSD causing traumas that are connected to you immediate home environment. If your trauma is not connected to immediate environment, but stems from an outside situation, then you have the advantage to easily establish a boundary separating the outside world from your home. Afterwards, transform your home into a most peaceful healing and secure space, where you can properly recover and manage the aftereffect of whatever trauma you experienced. No matter how you look at it, your peaceful and safe home space is absolutely essential to your healing progress.

FEELING SAFE, PROTECTED, RELAXED AND ABLE TO REFLECT, REST, AND FIND REFUGE FROM THE OUTSIDE WORLD IS AS ESSENTIAL AS AIR, OR WATER…IT IS ABSOLUTELY CRUCIAL TO YOUR HEALTH.

If you establish that kind of a healing oasis in at least a corner of one room, or entire house, it will offer you the space that you need. From there on, your can rebuild your strength and stamina to take on new challenges, liberate yourself from your PTSD completely, and hopefully launch a new chapter of your life.

ESOTERIC PERSPECTIVE

From the esoteric, subtle energy perspective, your physical environment has a certain vibration. If this vibration is unharmonious, it obviously affects your physical, mental and emotional body in unharmonious ways. If you live with challenging people that are part of your PTSD, there are invisible subtle energy cords that connect you and keep you in the unhealthy dynamic. Establishing your own safe space of peace, will help you sustain a strong zone of your own harmonious frequency, that will support your recharging ability, anytime you enter the safe-zone space. This is your way of detaching away from toxic environment and gaining strength in your own healthy frequency zone. Subtle frequencies have to resonate together, but the stronger frequency wins and overpowers the weaker one. If your harmonious frequency is stronger, it will win and eventually you will overrule the negative and maintain the positive frequency in your environment.

WHAT DOES YOUR FOOD HAVE TO DO WITH IT?

How you feed and care for your physical body, reveals a lot about how you feel about yourself and how in touch you are with your emotions. It also reveals about how you deal with your PTSD, and if the aftereffects have spilled into your eating habits. We are not going to talk extensively about diet, but it is obvious that proper nourishment is a vital part of your general state of well being. It is also a clear message to your body, about how much you care for it. If you deprive it of vibrant food, but overwhelm it with toxic food, your body does not feel loved and cared for, while not receiving help in maintaining optimal functionality.

Depriving yourself of healthy food, not making an effort to prepare your own food, sends a clear signal that you do not care about yourself, do not love yourself, and don't want to be bothered with the physical needs for managing proper nourishment.

It happens quite often that someone keeps complaining about how unwell they feel, yet they make absolutely no effort to improve their eating habits. They overeat, or simply eat bad food that offers them no nourishment, and actually damages their healthy system, creating a general feeling of un-wellness, depletion, depression and fatigue. Poor concentration, agitated disposition and low energy level are most often caused by poor eating habits.

UNLESS YOU TAKE CARE OF YOUR BODY, YOU CANNOT EXPECT TO FEEL VIBRANT, FULL OF ENERGY, AND LEAD A HAPPY AND FULFILLING LIFE.

Another aspect that is important to prevent, is addictive eating habits or overeating foods for comfort, while avoiding to face and recognize your unharmonious, unwell or unhealthy emotional state. Food can be a distraction, and an addiction that's often associated with PTSD aftereffects, that were perhaps never dealt with. Overeating to hide your physical attributes and envelop yourself in excess body mass is often the PTSD affect of abused or victimized young adults. They want to hide the physical body that was traumatized, so that they could prevent any future attacks.

Depression hiding in overeating, or lack of emotional support, fear and anxiety – these are countless causes of eating disorders, most often connected to an unresolved PTSD experience. The trauma may have happened in the past or is still ongoing, but nobody seems to want to address it or deal with it. Even if you don't have these specific situations, it is nevertheless very important to properly nurture your physical body on a daily basis. Ignoring and skipping meals, causes havoc in your system and with time various imbalances will get established, resulting in complex health ailments.

For example, sugar addiction when feeling down causes the unavoidable lack of energy and one can be in the spinning cycle that only grows in dysfunction, and while younger people can certainly avoid seeing the consequences as fast and clearly as older people, but nevertheless, they do eventually manifest and may take quite a while to overcome. Once your physical system adjusts to the unhealthy lifestyle, certain habits and addictions are formed and with time they accumulate and establish unhealthy patterns in your physical body.

Healthy nutritional habits are an absolute must. Even more so in today's world, where we are surrounded by food that can be practically toxic to a sensitive system. It does matter and is essential to be involved and pay close attention to what you consume, where your food is bought, how is it prepared, and what combinations and amounts you select.

IT IS DIFFICULT TO IMAGINE OVERCOMING ANY KIND OF PTSD IF YOU AVOID AND SKIP PROPER NUTRITION.

Why? Because your body will have to make up for the imbalance caused by bad eating habits and the consequences will spill over into your physical general sense of well being, your mental and emotional state, your resilience to fight off viruses, and certainly to maintain your energy level. If you feel lethargic and want to create a new healthy lifestyle, it will be very challenging, and almost impossible. If you feel depressed, because you are simply depleted as a result of your poor diet, you will not have the stamina or energy to establish a new healthy lifestyle and overcome old PTSD elements that a company you into today. Eating well, properly, healthy and appropriate for your specific needs is a clear signal to your body that you care, and can be loving, kind, tender with it, while you appreciate everything that it does for you.

How much clearer of a message can you send to your physical self – your precious body? The other important new healthy habit that is tied to proper eating habits is that you actually begin paying attention to how you feel, what foods agree with you, are healthier, make you feel your very best, and offer you the energy and vital source that you need.

Are you at all aware if you don't feel well after a meal? Do you examine if something you ate was maybe not the best choice? You have to find these food selections individually, as we are all different and it simply doesn't mean that if food is organic it will agree with you or even be a best choice for your specific system. Organic chocolate or organic salad are two different foods and perhaps one or both doesn't agree with your sensitive digestive system. But yet, they are both organic. I often hear people completely dismissing they may be eating wrong food. They state; " Everything I eat is organic, so my diet is very good." The truth is, you may be consuming the wrong combination, or wrong food, despite the fact that it's organic. Yes, finding the ideal diet for yourself requires effort, work and developing attunement with your body, so you understand how certain foods affect you. Inform yourself about the food you consume, and learn a new habit of preparing the food yourself with your own hands.

Is all the food you eat prepared by someone else? Why? Are you simply too lazy to learn the very basics? And if you do cook and have a large family, do you cook for your needs as well, or just to accommodate everyone else, while your own dietary needs are ignored? You may think this is not important, but it is, more so than you realize. Show your body that you are paying attention to its needs, understand what messages it is sending to you, and discover what is the ideal eating pattern for you, not only your relatives, or whatever is on the menu at the local restaurant where you eat.

EATING IS A VERY INTIMATE ACT AND WHATEVER YOU CONSUME, LEAVES TRACES OF SUBTLE ENERGY WITHIN YOU.

Vibrant food will leave you vibrant, whereas processed food will weigh you down. Eating is not an automatic task, a useless everyday activity. Take the time to respect and pay attention to properly care for your amazing body that serves you through your entire life. Be aware about its needs and begin a healthy empowering eating habit today.

ESOTERIC PERSPECTIVE

From the subtle energy perspective, the traumatized aura creates a subtle protective shield so thick and dense, that it actually eventually turns into physical mass in the form of gained weight. Quite often excessive weight gain is a direct, unrecognized consequence of PTSD. It can also manifest in the opposite way, with eating disorders and extreme weight loss – the subtle energy body is so depleted, that it is losing its ability for self-defense. All these physical manifestations are clear signs of silent suffering, and subtle energy imbalance. Pay attention to your body and consciously support its needs, so it can serve you well.

YOUR DAILY ACTIVITIES

This is another very important area of your life. What kind of activities fill your days?

Apart from making a living and tending to your various family obligations, are you finding time for activities that inspire you, help you relax, decompress? Do you meditate and connect to your intuition? Are you making life choices that agree with you and serve your best interest?

No matter how many obligations await, you will not be doing yourself or anyone else any favors, if you deny your basic needs for enough sleep, rest, and recovery from high stress activities that you may be encountering.

How does this relate to PTSD?

On one hand you may be escaping into workaholic mode just to ignore your PTSD that keeps persisting in your life. Perhaps this is a distraction to help you ignore your inner feelings, or perpetual pressure you put on yourself.

> **EXAMINE YOUR MOTIVATION FOR ALL YOUR DAILY ACTIVITIES. HOW MANY OF THEM DO YOU GENUINELY ENJOY?**

Any activity that you choose should be ideally done with enthusiasm and some level of enjoyment. Of course the majority of people have to work in situations that do not necessarily inspire them. However, when the workday is completed, your after-work activities should contain some level of respite. This will help establish a nice balance that will support your PTSD recovery.

ESOTERIC PERSPECTIVE

From the subtle energy perspective, a healthy lifestyle helps keep your energy body strong and resilient to ongoing challenges. In connection with PTSD, healthy activities will help restore your natural harmonious frequency and re-establish your original natural healthy state of functioning.

YOUR SUPPORT SYSTEM

Now that we have covered the basics of your own individual lifestyle and self-care, we are ready to address the next very crucial and decisive element in your life that plays a very important role. On your path to recovery from PTSD there is one indisputably important aspect that will make a significant difference. That is your support system. These are the people, family, friends, experts and if necessary – your therapists, that you surround yourself with throughout your life.

Let's keep in mind as we said before, that most often your PTSD is connected to some event or experience involving another person or persons. Even in situations where you were alone during a traumatic experience, there will often be another person somehow connected to your trauma. Even if the other person played an overall positive role, they remind you of what happened. However, this person may later become an important part of your healing process or support system, while helping you work through the remains of your PTSD. You feel a sense of trust connected to them, because they have a unique perspective and can understand you, since they were present during your ordeal. Your immediate family members can also be a close support system, unless they were involved in causing your PTSD. While immediate family dynamics are complex, the family members can often suffer from their own PTSD experience, as it relates to your own trauma.

For example: if you had an accident that caused you PTSD, your immediate family is also affected and has their own PTSD related to your accident. Therefore, their support may be limited, as they themselves need some healing as well. Your friends can be an excellent source of support, however your friends should not, and cannot replace a qualified professional therapist.

> **YOUR FRIENDS MAY CARRY THEIR OWN PTSD,
> OR CHARACTER TRAITS, INCLINATIONS, JUDGMENTS,
> BLAME, GUILT AND PERSONAL DISPOSITIONS,
> THAT MAY NOT BE HELPFUL IN YOUR DEALING WITH YOUR PTSD.
> INSTEAD OF BURDENING A FRIEND, SEEK THE HELP OF A THERAPIST.**

Your friends may not be able to deeply understand all complex elements that come into play with your PTSD, or may suggest solutions that may not be helpful and could cause even more ongoing trauma for you. Finally, it is important to address the possibility of professional help that could help you overcome the most burdensome and overwhelming challenges of PTSD. If the consequences of trauma are preventing you from leading a healthy life and interfere with your basic life's activities, you should seek help from a healthcare professional. In addition, you can use various complementary healing modalities that will help the effectiveness of various traditional therapeutic methods. Here I want to mention again, that Mudras are a complementary healing modality and will compliment any kind of healing approach you are using. A traditional approach of allopathic medicine, or an alternative approach with use of homeopathy or other alternative methods – all these modalities work in harmony with Mudras. Your support system is your immediate energy backing that will help catch you when you feel challenged, overwhelmed, or are experiencing a crisis. It is important to know that you're not alone and isolated, but have a strong support system in place, so you can always count on their unconditional love.

ESOTERIC PERSPECTIVE

Unless they are the cause of your PTSD, your friends and family who lovingly support you, are compatible with your natural subtle frequency and help you maintain a powerful and healing energy field, that recharges you and protects you from outside negative influences. Together you are stronger and more resilient.

REGAINED INTEREST AND PURPOSE

No matter what state of your PTSD healing process you find yourself in, one of the most powerful and effective healing aspects is your continued engagement with activities that interest you, and keep you aligned with your purpose and your life's desires. This way, you maintain a strong positive habit and prevent PTSD from negatively impairing the life you deserve and desire. Keeping up with healthy activities, continuing to pursue your goals and moving on, will help create a sense of space and distance between you and the past traumatic event, and help you experience new, positive and happy events that will confirm your ability to recover, and move forward with your life. Allowing yourself to remain paralyzed with past fear or trauma, will keep you stagnant and increase the hardship of re-engaging in the activities of regular life and regaining a sense of normalcy.

REVISIT AND REFLECT UPON YOUR PURSUITS, DESIRES AND WISHES YOU HAD BEFORE THE TRAUMATIC EVENT, AND CONTINUE PURSUING THEM IN WHATEVER WAY YOU CAN.

If the traumatic event has somewhat limited or completely eliminated your previous purpose, desire or ambition, this will need more work and exploration, as to how you can continue on your life's path, but perhaps in a different direction.

An example would be a sportsman who loses their career, resulting from a serious injury. This is certainly going to leave them with some deep and challenging PTSD, however the resilient human spirit will help them find a new path, that may be just as rewarding and perhaps even more meaningful, than the short lived and very competitive sporting career that has its obvious human limitations.

NATURAL HEALING MODALITIES

Any natural and holistic path that will help soothe your physical, mental and emotional pain, help you heal your overall state, can and should be explored. However, since we are all different, you need to find your unique personal preferences that appeal and work with your very specific and unique needs. This pursuit is also an important element in your establishing an optimally healing environment. Mudras are a powerful magnifier of your subtle energy field and help remove the unhealthy energy patterns, cords and unharmonious energy density, that prevents you from healthy and optimal functioning. In the pursuit of healing your PTSD, in this chapter you will find Mudras that will help you establish a nurturing and peaceful healing space, for optimal receptivity and progress of your mission.

SELF-KINDNESS AND SELF-COMPASSION

On a final note, no matter how much or little of active engagement you can manage, when creating a healing and harmonious environment for yourself, the one element that supersedes all, is how you behave and treat yourself. All the elements we addressed that facilitate a healing process and help you speed the way to full recovery, will be expedited when you learn to practice self-kindness and self-compassion. These are your intentional positive actions to support and pursue your healthy disposition towards yourself, your past, and your future.

No ONE CAN SUBSTITUTE THE HEALTHY SELF-LOVE YOU NEED.

This is a necessary ability in order to develop an independent, strong and healthy mindset, so that you take a conscious step out of the victim mode, and shift your position into becoming and reclaiming yourself as a winning, resilient, and successful individual.

YOUR ASSIGNMENT

AFFIRMATION

> ## MY HEALTHY, SAFE HOME AND
> ## STRONG SUPPORT SYSTEM IS HELPING ME HEAL

DIARY

In this chapter you are recognizing the importance of maintaining a healthy and supportive environment and lifestyle. It is an essential part of your recovery and healing process, that you have a safe haven, where you can deal with your emotional states, release the old, and welcome the new healthy and confident disposition.

PROCESS

Work thru the questions, come back in a few days, see if anything changed, add it on, clarify and self-discover through the process.

PRACTICE

This week is about establishing a supportive and healthy home base, work area and finding a loving and kind support system. Examine your current situation and see where you could make improvements. Pay attention to what kind of energy, order or disarray, and general atmosphere you allow to surround you. Make a conscious effort to energetically uplift and cleanse your home. Use sage to cleanse energy. Next, review your eating habits and examine how that affects your overall sense of wellbeing. And lastly, diligently review the kind of people you surround yourself with: do they offer support, or do they expect you to support them? Are they present when you need them, or they seem to disappear?

Be realistic about their intentions, interests and reliability, criticism or unconditional friendship and support. Do they enable your bad habits, or help keep you accountable for your choices and consequences? Establish a positive, fair and most reliable support system of family, friends, and people that truly have your best interest at heart. You're better off having just a few true friends, than an army of false ones.

YOUR HOME, FOOD, LIFESTYLE CHOICES AND SUPPORT SYSTEM
ARE THE BACKBONE OF YOUR LIFE.
MAINTAIN THEM WITH CARE AND LOVE.

CREATE YOUR HEALING SPACE

1. DO YOU HAVE A HEALING HOME ENVIRONMENT?

2. WHAT COULD YOU CHANGE TO IMPROVE IT?

3. DO YOU HAVE A CHALLENGING WORK ENVIRONMENT?

4. ARE YOU EATING HEALTHY AND ARE YOU PREPARING YOUR OWN FOOD?

5. ARE YOU ENGAGED IN HEALTHY LIFESTYLE ACTIVITIES?

6. DO YOU HAVE A STRONG SUPPORT SYSTEM?

7. ARE YOU CLEAR ABOUT AND ARE PURSUING YOUR LIFE PURPOSE?

8. DO YOU PRACTICE SELF-KINDNESS AND SELF-COMPASSION?

MUDRA FOR TRUST

Sit with a straight back and keep your shoulders down, nice and relaxed. Place your right hand on top and over the back of the left hand. Lift your arms up, stretched up and above your head, creating a circle. Press the thumb tips together and visualize a protective circle of white light surrounding you. Hold this energy strong and unwavering in your mind and sense a soothing calmness overcome your entire being. Trust that you are shielded in the field of Universal protection. Practice for three minutes. Men hold a reversed position, the left palm on top of right.

BREATH
FAST, SHORT BREATH OF FIRE FROM NAVEL

MANTRA
HAR HAR HAR WAHE GURU
(God's Creation, His supreme power and Wisdom)

CHAKRA
CROWN - 7

HEALING COLOR
VIOLET

AFFIRMATION

I TRUST THE UNIVERSE LOVES AND PROTECTS ME

MUDRA FOR HEALING A BROKEN HEART

Sit with a straight back and keep your shoulders down, nice and relaxed. Gently hold the hands together and lift them up in front of your face, with the tips of the middle fingers pointing towards the Third Eye area. Your hands are touching your face, the thumbs are placed around your nose and mouth. Leave some space between the little fingers and breathe through this opening. Hold for Three minutes then relax.

BREATH
LONG, DEEP AND SLOW AS IF DRINKING WATER THRU THE SPACE
BETWEEN PALMS AND THE OPENING BETWEEN LITTLE FINGERS

MANTRA
HUMME HUM HUM BRAHAM
(Calling Upon Your Infinite Self))

CHAKRAS
HEART - 4, THROAT - 5, THIRD EYE - 6

HEALING COLORS
GREEN, BLUE, INDIGO

AFFIRMATION

MY BREATH CAN HEAL AND SOOTHE MY HEART

MUDRA for Opening your Heart center

Sit with a straight back and keep your shoulders down, nice and relaxed. Lift your hands up in front of your heart and create a cup, palms facing each other, all fingers spread out and pointing up. Only the upper parts of your thumbs and pinkies and the bases of your palms are touching. Visualize opening your heart, keeping fingers outstretched. Hold for Three minutes and relax.

BREATH
LONG, DEEP AND SLOW THRU YOUR NOSE

MANTRA
SAT NAM
(Truth Is God's Name, One in Spirit)

CHAKRA
HEART - 4

HEALING COLOR
GREEN

AFFIRMATION

I AM READY TO OPEN MY HEART

MUDRA FOR SELF ~ CONFIDENCE

Sit with a straight back, shoulders down, nice and relaxed. Lift your hands up to the level of your solar plexus with elbows bent to the sides. Bend the middle, ring, and little fingers of each hand and align them back to back. Extend and press the index fingertips together and extend and press the thumb tips together. The thumbs are pointed towards you and the index fingers away from you. Hold for Three minutes, then relax.

BREATH
LONG, DEEP AND SLOW THRU YOUR NOSE

MANTRA
EK ONG KAR SAT GURU PRASAD, SAT GURU PRASAD EK ONG KAR
(The Creator Is the One That Dispels Darkness and Illuminates Us by His Grace)

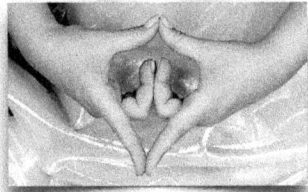

CHAKRAS
SOLAR PLEXUS - 3, THIRD EYE - 6

HEALING COLORS
YELLOW, INDIGO

AFFIRMATION
I AM READY, WILLING AND ABLE TO ACCOMPLISH MY GOALS

MUDRA FOR PROTECTION

Sit with a straight back, shoulders down, nice and relaxed. Place both hands on your upper chest, and cross your left hand over the right one. Palms are facing you and all fingers are together. Hold for Three minutes.

BREATH
LONG, DEEP AND SLOW THRU YOUR NOSE

MANTRA
OM

(God in His Absolute State)

CHAKRAS
ALL

HEALING COLORS
ALL

AFFIRMATION

THE DIVINE LIGHT IS MY EVERLASTING PROTECTOR

Week Six

REPLACE NEGATIVE WITH POSITIVE

This chapter will open up a new area of your deeper sense of self. We have covered much and yet, where we are going now, we have not been before. You are ready. The questions you will ask yourself may seem quite easy – on the surface that is. However, in your depths, they hold much power, and often hide, pretending to be something else entirely.

I am talking about your current, ever prevailing emotions. Not the emotions displayed on the surface that we throw around in easy going conversations, but the emotions that are so deeply ingrained in you, that they have become an essential part of you. You may have not noticed that they have taken a hold of your entire perception field, and have become deep rooted in you to such an extent, that they became you.

If you are going through a difficult period in your life and are enveloped in deep sadness, your entire perception of life will shift, and you will see everything through the eyes veiled in this sad condition. Likewise, if you are angry, your anger will spread over your other, more pleasant sides of your personality, and will overpower them to such an extent, that you may see the entire world as an angry place.

EVERY POWERFUL EMOTION COLORS YOUR PERCEPTION.

On a positive note, if you are in love, it will seem to you that the world is beautiful, people are kind, and everyone is happy. But in fact, you will be the one feeling the power of love and your perception will be affected in such a way, that you will believe everyone else is also permeated with emotions that you feel.

Maintaining a very neutral perception, where your emotional state does not taint or hinder your observation of the world that surrounds you, requires maturity, wisdom and impeccable ability to discern. This way you are not overly affected by anything that happens, since you know it is a passing state, good or bad for that matter. This grants you enormous resilience in face of great challenges or turmoil. In happier times, you certainly enjoy them, but are never losing your head or becoming engulfed in the trappings of the earthly illusion.

In regard to PTSD, this presents an important ability, because you will be able to overcome the trauma and find wisdom, perhaps even great gifts in your past challenging experiences. We will explore that a bit later, but here and now, we shall focus on your emotions – as you are feeling today. We are all human and can be overwhelmed by various events that affect our perception, at least to a certain degree.

Your memory of a certain geographical location may seem beautiful, simply because you experienced some beautiful adventures while you were there in person. So your perception is intensely connected to those emotional experiences. Likewise if an experience was unpleasant, you will associate the geographical location with that memory, which will taint it for you. Your memory of feelings plays an enormous role in how you experience life and allow the past to affect your present and future. Which leads us to the current time and place, your feelings right here and now, and how they affect everything you are experiencing in your life. PTSD leaves traces of emotions that are not pleasant. The emotions connected to trauma are most often fear, anger, rage, abandonment, loss, grief and similar states, all creating a heaviness in your general disposition and perception of life. Now we are actively engaging in healing your challenging emotional state and creating a new space for opening to positive, pleasant and happier emotional conditions.

IF THE NEGATIVE STATE IS OVERWHELMING, THERE WILL BE NO SPACE FOR SOMETHING HAPPY TO COME INTO YOUR LIFE.

Of course, you can't just easily shift your emotional state and replace it by selecting a better, and more pleasant one. You need to recognize your unhappy or generally negative condition, and understand it from various sides. Reflecting on all the facts and circumstances as an objective observer, will help you dissolve a burdening self-perception of a victim and relieve some of that negative pressure. Once that is accomplished, you can consciously allow for release of the past – while immediately replacing your new space of emotional receptivity with something you select that is substantially healthier, more optimistic, positive, constructive, and will make way for new positive experiences.

> **YOU HAVE TO MAKE A CONSCIOUS DECISION THAT YOU ARE READY, WILLING AND ABLE TO MOVE FORWARD AND AWAY FROM THE PAST.**

Your mind plays a big role in this process, for it will help you understand your past, reason with your consciousness, and solidify a resolution that you are ready to overcome your current stuck state of PTSD induced negativity.

CONSCIOUS BELIEF SYSTEM NEUTRALIZATION

This process begins with deep awareness of how you actually feel at this very moment. You would be surprised about how many people are so removed and alienated from their own feelings or inner awareness, that they don't even know how they feel. They look unhappy, anxious, but they don't ever stop for a moment and take a look at themselves to recognize what is happening. They are practically sleep-walking through life, for perhaps the truth would be unbearable and would overwhelm them. It may hurt too much and in desperate attempt to suffocate it, they turn to other, numbing and addictive habits, activities and perhaps even serious addictions. But when you are ready to take a moment and look within, to recognize how you feel, the next big question appears: why do you feel this way?

Many of us have no idea why we feel a certain way, until we carefully examine our own disposition. What will force or inspire you to do that?
Perhaps a breaking point, a shift in consciousness, a life-altering event. Whatever it is, when you are ready, you will see it loud and clear and it won't necessarily be easy, but it will be a relief and the beginning of a profoundly healing process.

> **YOU CAN'T HEAL YOUR EMOTIONS, UNTIL YOU KNOW HOW YOU FEEL.**

Until that realization, your unexpressed emotions may come out as a burst of anger, jealousy, envy, or meanness, when in fact it all truly stems from grief. But because you can't express it, it manifests in a different, aggressive, lashing-out way. Grief doesn't make you lash out, but suppressed grief does. Sadness doesn't make you angry, but suppressed sadness can make you behave in all sorts of unpleasant ways. Fear itself is very specific if you express it, but if you pretend it's not there, and cover it in pride, shame, guilt and denial, the emotional display will be very different. It may be aggression, or violence, all because a general sense of fear has exploded and found an expressive outlet in a different presentation of your behavior.

This is one of the reasons why you need to discover your true authentic feelings of the moment. Now, let's begin examining your emotions, so that you can consciously address them, and then willfully transform them.

IF YOU ADMIT THAT YOU ARE ANGRY, THE ANGER WILL EASILY DIFFUSE. IF YOU HIDE AND DENY IT, IT WILL FESTER.

Expressing your feelings is always healthier than silence. However, once you do identify them, silence becomes your ally. In silence and quietly reflective time, you can being to process them, and consciously and willfully transform them into a healing, positive and beneficial emotional state. Your thoughts resonate, and a positive mindset will help you establish, maintain and cultivate a healthy personal frequency. This is our goal.

HOW DO YOU FEEL?

This is a very revealing exercise that will help you get in touch with your deep emotional state and begin the self-motivated process of healing. There are many emotional charts out there, most of them have similarities, however some emotions are often simply missing. I have composed for you a detailed "emotional review" to help examine and find your emotional states. Make a step forward to harmonize them and find a peaceful, joyful and optimistic state of inner and outer balance. Review the many emotional states that are interconnected and play a decisive role in how you experience your everyday life.

EMOTIONS OF FEAR

Frightened	Inadequate	Insignificant	Threatened
Insecure	Inferior	Embarrassed	Helpless
Anxious	Worthless	Ashamed	Worried
Vulnerable	Insignificant	Startled	Bewildered
Scared	Excluded	Confused	Discouraged
Submissive	Persecuted	Astonished	Shocked
Weak	Nervous	Distracted	Dismayed
Rejected	Exposed	Overwhelmed	Disillusioned

EMOTIONS OF PEACE

Peaceful	Responsive	Thoughtful	Secure
Trusting	Serene	Intimate	Confident
Assured	Thankful	Relaxed	Content
Hopeful	Nurturing	Pensive	

The opposite of fear are emotions of peace. Examine all these options and see if any of them apply to your general feelings, that seem to be a part of your emotional fabric. Now replace a negative feeling from the FEAR column, with a new, selected positive feeling from the PEACE column.

Take your time, and select a desirable positive emotional state.
For example: if you are feeling helpless, find the counter remedy emotion of trust. Trust is your new selected emotion that you consciously choose to cultivate. You can affirm this choice with a positive affirmation:
"I choose to trust in life and the Universe."

EMOTIONS OF SADNESS

These are emotions that give us a sense of heaviness and helpless passivity. See if you find any emotions that seem to resonate with what you are experiencing.

Sad	Guilty	Inferior	
Lost	Disappointed	Isolated	
Depressed	Ashamed	Apathetic	
Pain	Lonely	Empty	
Hurt	Bored	Sleepy	Abandoned
Grief	Tired	Vulnerable	Victimized
Sorrow	Remorseful	Despair	Fragile
Unhappy	Stupid	Hurt	Powerless
			Embarrassed

EMOTIONS OF HAPPINESS

The opposite side of sadness is a sense of happiness. Examine how these manifestations of that feeling contribute to your general profile:

Happy	Excited	Free	Sensitive
Playful	Grateful	Curious	Intimate
Content	Sensuous	Inquisitive	Inspired
Interested	Joyful	Successful	Daring
Proud	Energetic	Confident	Fascinating
Accepted	Cheerful	Respected	Stimulating
Powerful	Creative	Valued	Amused
Trusting	Hopeful	Courageous	Playful
Optimistic	Aroused	Loving	Blessed
Ecstatic	Cheeky	Thankful	

Examine all these options and see if any of them apply to your general feelings, that seem to be a part of your emotional fabric. Now replace a negative feeling from the SAD column, with a new, selected positive feeling from the HAPPY column. Take your time, and select a desirable positive emotional state. For example: if you are feeling depressed, find the counter remedy emotion of gratitude. Gratitude is your new selected emotion that you consciously choose to cultivate. You can affirm this choice with a positive affirmation:
"I am grateful for all the blessings in my life."

CHOOSE YOUR NEW FUTURE

Whatever your emotional state is, now you have a good clear view of how you feel. It is very different when you just sit fuming away, or when you face it and admit to yourself that you are angry, or sad…and then explore further what brought you there and what caused your feelings. This gives you the amazing opportunity to consciously select the positive counter-effect emotion and explore various aspects of your life, that could help you reactivate the more positive, healthy and happier feelings. For example: if you discover that you feel fearful, the opposite of that would be empowered. Now in the column with all the empowering feelings, find one that is possible for you to evoke. This feeling will help you return back onto the positive side of the spectrum. If you suffer from sadness, you can select a joyful emotion that seems possible for you at the moment; for example… gratitude.

Consciously selecting to recognize the gratitude within yourself for something in your life that is truly a gift – precisely this action will help you distance yourself from the negative emotions and find a way to turn things around.

EMOTIONS OF ANGER

These are emotions that deplete our energy field and bind us to others. See if any emotions seem to resonate with what you are experiencing now:

Anger	Annoyed	Sarcastic	
Let down	Hateful	Distant	Provoked
Humiliated	Selfish	Betrayed	Infuriated
Bitter	Envious	Resentful	Withdrawn
Mad	Hostile	Disrespected	Numb
Aggressive	Hurt	Ridiculed	Dismissive
Frustrated	Skeptical	Indignant	Violated
Distant	Irritated	Jealous	Furious

EMOTIONS OF LOVE

One of the opposite sides of anger is Love. Examine how these manifestations of that feeling contribute to your general profile:

Love	Good spirited	Tender	
Constancy	Desire	Loyal	
Ecstasy	Interest	Inclusive	Elation
Attractive	Enthusiasm	Euphoric	Union
Affection	Devotion	Joy	Like
Adoration	Generous	Awe	Sympathy
Sharing	Giving	Hope	Optimism
Exhilaration	Protected	Gentle	Empathy
Connected	Compassion	Sweet	Interest
Caring	Passion	Kind	
Feel good	Nurturing	Delight	

Examine all these options and see if any of them apply to your general feelings that seem to be a part of your emotional fabric. Now replace a negative feeling from the ANGER column, with a new, selected positive feeling from the LOVE column. Take your time, and select a desirable positive emotional state. For example: if you are feeling jealous, find the counter remedy emotion of compassion. This is your new selected emotion that you consciously choose to cultivate. You can affirm this choice with a positive affirmation:
"I feel compassion towards others and myself."

CHOOSE YOUR NEW DISPOSITION TOWARDS RELATIONSHIPS

Your relationships are incredible opportunities to learn about yourself, your purpose, and your ability to interact, relate, share, give-take, and of course... love. If you find yourself in a congested field of personally negative or more depleted emotional states, you cannot in any way expect to attract or sustain a happy, healthy and stimulating relationship. You make up half of that relationship and nobody can sustain a partnership on their own. It does take two and you can only do so much. Reestablish a healthy give-and-take balance and observe how your new established healthy emotional disposition creates a positive chain reaction within all your relationships.

CHOOSE YOUR NEW CALLING

Now you are in a perfect place to reexamine your calling, your life's mission, and various pursuits. If you dreamed about an endeavor through your very early life and circumstances prevented you from pursuing it, now that you are reprograming your disposition towards how you absorb, observe and react to your life's events...this may all begin to shift for you in a big way. Releasing your PTSD emotional leftovers will give you ample space for new a disposition, ambition, pursuits and opening a new field of possibilities.

> **WHEN YOUR PERCEPTION EXPANDS,**
> **SO DO YOUR LIFE'S OPPORTUNITIES.**
> **LIMITATIONS VANISH AND HORIZONS OPEN UP.**

EMOTIONS OF FEELING BAD

These are emotions that keep you in a general state of unhappiness and discontent. See if you find any emotions that seem to resonate with what you are experiencing:

Bored	Overwhelmed	Awful	
Busy	Out of control	Repelled	Revolted
Stressed	Sleepy	Averse	Nauseated
Tired	Unfocused	Repulsive	Detestable
Indifferent	Disgust	Contempt	Horrified
Apathetic	Shame	Guilty	Humiliated
Pressured	Awkward	Judgmental	
Hesitant	Disapproving	Embarrassed	
Rushed	Disappointed	Appalled	

EMOTIONS OF SELF-ACCEPTANCE & EMPOWERMENT

The opposite side of the spectrum are feelings of self-empowerment. Examine how these manifestations of feelings contribute to your general profile:

Faithful	Confident	Encouraged	
Important	Discerning	Empowered	Excited
Appreciated	Valuable	In Awe	Optimistic
Respected	Worthwhile	Eager	Enthusiastic
Proud	Successful	Energetic	
Aware	Surprised	Amazed	

Examine all these options and see if any of them apply to your general feelings that seem to be a part of your emotional fabric. Now replace a negative feeling from the FEELING BAD column, with a new, selected positive feeling from the EMPOWERING column. Take your time, and select a desirable positive emotional state. For example: if you are feeling overwhelmed, find the counter remedy emotion of confidence and awareness. This is your new selected emotion that you consciously choose to cultivate. You can affirm this choice with a positive affirmation: *"I am aware and confident of my actions and abilities."*

CHOOSE YOUR NEW LIFESTYLE

Once you consciously decide in what positive direction you can direct your new life projections, your view will certainly change. Like we mentioned before – if you see everything through the veil of sadness, the world will be sad. If you find reasons for gratitude, the world will seem like a blessing. This is a very empowering technique to divert back onto the path you want to travel on. And what happens next, is the inner-knowing that you are choosing how to live your life, how to relate to everything that has happened to you in the past, is happening to you at this very moment, and consequentially how it will manifest in the future. Now you make the biggest change:

> **YOU ARE READY TO MAKE A DECISIVE SHIFT —**
> **YOU CEASE TO REMAIN LIKE A HELPLESS OBSERVER**
> **AND BECOME A CONSCIOUS AND ACTIVE PARTICIPANT IN YOUR LIFE.**

You are not helpless, weak, vulnerable and easily defeated. You are in fact the opposite. You are empowered, aware and safe, making choices that will alter your feelings, perception and ultimately improve your life. This will be the basis for your new lifestyle pattern, where you triumph over whatever trauma and PTSD you are suffering from. An act of empowerment is recognizing your present feelings, and clarifying how you want to improve your emotional and overall state. It may be that you will have to search deep within to remember feelings of love, tenderness or healthy interpersonal interactions. But somewhere inside, you will make space to implant the healthy disposition and remove and abolish the old. You will consciously replace the negative with the positive emotional patterns. You are in charge.

CHOOSE YOUR NEW INTERESTS

Now a new sense of freedom enters your life. Remembering what brought you joy in the past will play a crucial role. It may have been piano playing when you were a child, it may have been drawing lessons, or whatever else brought you happiness and inspired you. It is certainly never too late for healing, especially if the person in question desires to do so. In relation to PTSD, by following your joyful and more positive experiences in life, you are depleting and incapacitating the subtle energy feed that is attached to your past, and are consciously directing it to feel and nurture something that is more pleasant, productive, and certainly incomparably healthier. Awareness of your feelings grants you the greatest gift – being able to free yourself from unwanted emotions and pursue your life's interests. You can recognize your aspirations by enthusiasm, joy, inspiration and a source of empowerment when engaging in activities, or pursuits that you love. Remember, your healthy and persistent ancient desire that you carry within your soul matrix, is something you can and should follow.

Why? Because it is a certain part of your life's mission and will remain a desire until it is fulfilled. Positive desires like helping others, nurturing a family, creating helpful opportunities for others, sharing your gifts whatever they may be…these desires are partially the reasons why you came back into this life. Pursuing your life's desires is something that is encouraged, since ignoring them won't make them go away, it will simply make them dormant and temporarily forgotten. But they will not evaporate into nothingness.

A DESIRE WILL LIVE WITHIN YOUR ENERGY MATRIX UNTIL IT RECEIVES AN OPPORTUNITY TO BE EXPERIENCED AND FULFILLED.

It is in your highest spiritual evolutionary interest that you recognize, acknowledge and pursue the hidden gifts you possess and share them with the world to create feelings of joy, peace and love.

CHOOSE YOUR NEW PURPOSE

And finally, the most asked question is always this:
"What is my purpose? What should I do? Why am I here?"

Well, now that you've reconstructed your emotional state and made it more pleasant and empowering, you can easily allow the information to come into your life, that will help guide you in the direction of helping you fulfill your purpose. All these possibilities lie ahead when you change your emotional state and consequently expand your perception. Fears limit us, but empowered emotional states infuse us with vibrant creative energy, that is like a tireless engine moving forward and driving us through the kind of life we've always wished for and dreamed of.

YOUR ASSIGNMENT
AFFIRMATION

EMOTIONS OF PEACE, HAPPINESS AND LOVE ARE HELPING ME ESTABLISH AND ENJOY VIBRANT HEALTH

DIARY

In this Chapter you are recognizing your emotional states. This is of crucial importance, for once you actually know and claim your true feelings, you immediately gain the ability to adjust them, even eliminate them, but preferably you learn to replace them with a counter-positive feeling. Yes, it is challenging to adjust how you feel, but it can be done in a most constructive way. You actually have to find the counter-positive emotion and search for situations, persons, activities and surroundings that help you evoke the positive emotional state. If you feel more cheerful while surrounded by friends, you can reach out and communicate with friends. If this helps you, consciously engage in activities that you know for certain will help you implement the positive feeling. If you feel depressed while cooped up inside, but thrive in nature – you know what to do. You have a clear pathway to identify and engage in activities that will help you overcome the negative emotional states and establish new, happier ones. This is of crucial importance, so that you can move out of victim mode and gain a confident, lighter and happier disposition.

PROCESS

Work thru the questions, come back in a few days, see if anything changed, add it on, clarify and self-discover through the process.

PRACTICE

This week is about working with your emotions. You may feel different moods during the day, and each time become aware why you feel the way you do, what affects you the most, and how vulnerable you are to shifts in environment or other people's behavior. Ideally, your mood should remain stable, with comfortable fluctuations, and nothing should throw you off balance. Work towards it and become your own best and most reliable source of happiness and peace.

YOUR EMOTIONS OF INNER HAPPINESS AND PEACE, WILL HELP YOU ENJOY LIFE'S OFFERINGS.

GET IN TOUCH WITH YOUR FEELINGS

1. DO YOU FEEL FEARFUL? WHAT IS THE CAUSE?

2. DO YOU FEEL INNER PEACE? WHEN?

3. DO YOU FEEL SADNESS? WHAT IS THE CAUSE?

4. DO YOU FEEL HAPPY? WHEN ARE YOU THE HAPPIEST?

5. DO YOU FEEL ANGRY? WHAT IS THE CAUSE?

6. DO YOU FEEL LOVE? WHEN?

7. DO YOU HAVE ANY NEGATIVE FEELINGS? WHAT IS THE CAUSE?

8. DO YOU FEEL SELF-ACCEPTANCE?

9. DO YOU FEEL SELF-LOVE?

10. DO YOU FEEL DESERVING?

11. DO YOU FEEL GRATEFUL?

12. WHAT HELPS PROMOTE THESE POSITIVE FEELINGS?

MUDRA FOR DIMINISHING WORRY

Sit with a straight back, shoulders down, nice and relaxed. Bring the hands up in front of your heart with palms facing up. The sides of the little fingers and the inner sides of the palms are touching. Now bring your middle fingers tips together, and extend the thumbs away from the palms. Keep the fingers stretched as little antennas for energy. Hold for Three minutes, then relax and be still.

BREATH
LONG, DEEP AND SLOW THRU YOUR NOSE

CHAKRAS
HEART - 4, THROAT - 5, THIRD EYE - 6

HEALING COLORS
GREEN, BLUE, INDIGO

AFFIRMATION

I RELEASE ALL WORRY AND FEEL ASSURED

MUDRA FOR TRANQUILIZING YOUR MIND

Sit with a straight back, shoulders down, nice and relaxed. Bend your elbows and bring your hands up to your chest. Connect the middle fingertips and stretch them outward. Bend the rest of the fingers and press them together along the second joint. Connect your thumb tips and extend them toward you. Hold for Three minutes, then relax.

BREATH
LONG, DEEP AND SLOW THRU YOUR NOSE

MANTRA
MAN HAR TAN HAR GURU HAR

(Mind with God, Soul with God, the Divine Guide and His Supreme Wisdom)

CHAKRAS
SOLAR PLEXUS - 3, HEART - 4, THROAT - 5, THIRD EYE - 6

HEALING COLORS
YELLOW, GREEN, BLUE, INDIGO

AFFIRMATION

I AM SERENE, PEACEFUL AND TRANQUIL

MUDRA FOR SELF~IDENTIFICATION

Sit with a straight back and shoulders down, nice and relaxed. The left arm is at your waist, close to body, elbow bent at a 90° angle, and palm looking up towards the sky. The right arm is bent, close to body, and hand is brought up to shoulder level. Palm is facing down. The index and thumb fingertips are connected, the rest of the fingers are straight and together. Hold the Mudra and feel the energy interaction of the two palms and the balance it creates between your emotional and mental energies. Consciously expand the feeling of harmonious balance throughout your entire being. Hold for Three minutes, then relax.

BREATH
LONG, DEEP AND SLOW THRU YOUR NOSE
CHAKRAS
HEART - 4, THROAT - 5, THIRD EYE - 6, CROWN - 7
HEALING COLORS
GREEN, BLUE, INDIGO, VIOLET

AFFIRMATION

I PERCEIVE, RESPECT AND UNDERSTAND WHO I AM

MUDRA for STRONG CHARACTER

Sit with a straight back, shoulders down, nice and relaxed. Lift the right hand higher, closer to your mind, calling for mind-ego balance. Your left hand, connected to your heart is lower, closer to your heart. Palms are facing each other. Index fingers are pointing up, towards the sky. Practice for three minutes.

BREATH
LONG, DEEP AND SLOW THRU YOUR NOSE
MANTRA
HUMME HUM BRAHAM
(Calling on the Infinite Self)
CHAKRAS
SOLAR PLEXUS - 3, THIRD EYE - 6
HEALING COLORS
YELLOW, INDIGO

AFFIRMATION

I AM THE MASTER OF MY MIND

MUDRA FOR INNER INTEGRITY

Sit with a straight spine, shoulders down, nice long neck. Your upper arms are raised parallel to the ground, your elbows bent so your forearms are perpendicular. Bring your hands to ear level, palms out, facing forwards. Curl your fingers inward so that they touch the palms. Extend your thumbs straight out and point them toward your temples. Practice for at least three minutes, then relax.

BREATH
SHORT, FAST BREATH OF FIRE FROM NAVEL

MANTRA
SAT NAM

(Truth Is God's Name, One in Spirit)

CHAKRAS
SOLAR PLEXUS - 3, THIRD EYE - 6

HEALING COLORS
YELLOW, INDIGO

AFFIRMATION

I AM HONEST AND TRUE TO MYSELF
I UPHOLD MY INTEGRITY

MUDRA FOR CLOSING~OFF YOUR AURA

Sit with a straight back and keep your shoulders down, nice and relaxed. Bend your middle, ring and small fingers. Both index and thumb fingertips are extended and connected. Index fingertips are pointing towards the sky, thumbs towards the ground. Lift your hands up to the level of your throat. Hold for Three minutes and relax.

BREATH
LONG, DEEP AND SLOW THRU YOUR NOSE

MANTRA
OMM *(God in His Absolute State)*

CHAKRAS
ALL CHAKRAS

HEALING COLORS
ALL COLORS

AFFIRMATION

I CLOSE OFF MY AURA
MY INVISIBLE ENERGY SHIELD IS INDESTRUCTIBLE

Week Seven

REPROGRAMING Your CODES

The subtle energy codes are almost like fine energy programs that direct our general behavior. In fact, we all have countless codes embedded into our subtle bodies, that play a more or less decisive role in everything we do, and how we experience this life in its entirety.

The subtle energy codes are the vibrations of your expectations, assumptions, and self-imposed limitations that you live by. This isn't something you consciously decide about. It is something you are automatically accepting, as it unfolds in front of your very own eyes, from the first day of this life, onward.

**THE CODES DO NOT PERTAIN ONLY TO THIS LIFETIME.
THEY ARE WITH YOU THROUGH ETERNITY.**

How is that possible, you ask? If you were a very humble person in your past life, do you honestly believe that this time around you will be an ego blasting maniac? Hardly. Your code of humility shall follow you through the gates of eternity, and continue right into your current life.

Codes of your special gifts and talents are engrained in you, and you'll always feel a desire and deep longing to steer your life in the direction where they can be enjoyed, seen, used, experienced and further developed. You carry within you the past codes of success or failure, deep belief systems, expectations, as well as self-imposed limitations. You may think that codes are connected to karma. Well, everything is connected to your karmic file.

But it's not as cut and dry as you imagine. Codes are not your karma, they are your self-imposed limitations created by fears, or your courageous and brave dispositions, supported by patterns from your old belief system. Let's say you brought with you codes of incredible courage and bravery – this will help you tackle life's problems precisely that way – courageously and bravely.

You could say that codes are simply your own belief systems? Well, it's not as simple as that, because some belief systems get shaped by your upbringing, your parents, or the society that surrounds you in this particular life. And that can be substantially different from what you carry within your soul. However, this does not seal your fate and indicate that just because your parent's belief system was a certain way, you shall follow precisely in the same footsteps. Absolutely not.

Let's take an example of someone who is born into really dire circumstances, lives in desperate poverty, without any hope in sight for an even slight chance to escape and ascend to anything remotely successful in their life. Still, if this person possesses the codes of courage and success, they will leave their dire childhood environment, and build an amazing life for themselves – seemingly out of thin air. So how do you explain it? No-one was helping them, but here they are, completely overcoming and conquering their dire set-up, and living a storybook life that's entirely inspirational and extraordinary.

A PERSON CAN HAVE THE CODES FOR SUCCESS ORIGINATING IN THEIR FAR-AWAY PAST, AND MANIFEST THEM IN THIS PRESENT LIFETIME, NO MATTER HOW HOPELESS THE CIRCUMSTANCES IN CURRENT LIFE SEEM.

They will accomplish and ultimately master what their codes carry. This is the power of the codes. So in order to know who you are, and how you can create the life you want, while completely triumphing over any kind of PTSD, you need to recognize and understand your codes. And then what? Is this a hopeless case of being stuck with something seemingly out of your hands, or beyond your power to control it? No, not at all. You see, once you truly understand your codes, you are simultaneously gaining access to reprogram them, precisely as you wish. Because the moment you are aware of your restricting beliefs, expectations, assumptions and self-imposed limitations, the boundaries are suddenly broken, disassembled, busted, and irreparably changed.

It's like you are assuming that Santa Clause will deliver your gifts, and then you catch your parents placing the presents under the Christmas tree. They give up and reveal that Santa Clause in fact does not exist. There is no going back. Your Christmas present becomes the realization that your life has many more possibilities and much more potential than you ever imagined.

The question is: how content are you with your codes?
Do you want more out of your life, do you want to overcome all PTSD imposed limitations? Yes, you do. This means, the old codes must go.

PAST LIFE CODES EFFECT
ON YOUR PRESENT AND FUTURE

This is complicated, but also deeply fascinating. When you understand your own past-life codes, it feels like a gigantic door has opened and an entirely unknown and hidden magical room of your home is revealed. All this information within your being is actually accessible to you, but you need to dare to look deep inside and find it.

How can you uncover these codes? Whatever belief systems you have, that did NOT originate in your upbringing, through your parents, or been acquired later through your actions, the company you keep or society you live in – these are likely your old codes from long ago.

For example: if you have a strong urge to help the less privileged, but this particular topic was never present in anyone else around you, this is your personal old code. You are aware that people who are less privileged need our help AND that you can and want to help them. This is different from someone fearing poverty or perpetually assuming they will go poor, regardless of their financial situation. That kind of fear is a past life PTSD residue. But your generous and dedicated urge to help the poor, is something that is unique to you and is part of your old code. You could find quite a few possible old codes in your life, if you examine your deep-set beliefs and consequential actions that do not originate in your childhood, and can't be found in your immediate societal environment in this life. This way you can uncover, how your past life code has a direct effect on your current life.

YOUR CODE FOR PHYSICAL ABILITIES AND HEALTH

This is a very important code. It's about how you relate to your physical body, how resilient, strong, enduring or weak and fragile you believe to be.

Are you oblivious to your physical limitations?

Are you convinced you can withstand just about anything?

Do you believe you are immune to illness, are basically unbeatable, and will live forever?

Is your tendency to be a bit of a hypochondriac?

Are you fearful of suffering in physical pain caused by an illness?

Are you preoccupied by the prospect of inevitable death, regardless when?

Are you in tune with the realistic state of your physical body?

Are you out of touch, as to what shape you are in, and your general state of health?

Are you disconnected from your body, abusing it, and taking it for granted?

Are you mistreating your body and avoiding or ignoring healthy nutrition?

All these attitudes towards your physical self reveal a lot about you. The code of your own disposition towards your physical body significantly contributes and actually affects your state of health. Some people are completely ignorant of their physical needs, while others are obsessively preoccupied. They have a desperate need to cling to their youth and are incapable of accepting, enjoying, or even understanding the natural aging process.

How are you feeling and behaving in this department?

THE EXPECTATIONS YOU HAVE OF YOUR PHYSICAL BODY ARE ENCODED.

If your parents had a large family, and you were brought up encoded with the belief and expectation that you need to have a big family yourself, but you do not feel the same, or your body cannot fulfill this expectation, you may as a result feel like a failure, but in fact – it is the code that you carry, that was created in a combination of parental and societal pressure. If your parents were professional athletes and expect you to be one as well, this is a code you live with, yet you may prefer to be a scientist, far removed from any athletic activities. You may carry your own codes for amazing scientific abilities, that no one in your family does. So, you are the uniquely odd and different one in the family.

How do you handle the codes that relate to the conditions and abilities of your physical body? They can be oppressive, too demanding, confusing, or physically impossible to fulfill. Perhaps everyone in your immediate environment thrives on eating meat and drinking beer, yet you thrive by following a vegetarian diet. The code you are pressured to live by, is not in harmony with your own code of your physical body. On the other hand, if you grew up with everyone perpetually afraid of illness or physical exertion, or being too weak to engage in any kind of demanding physical activity, this is an example of a limiting code that will take some effort to overcome.

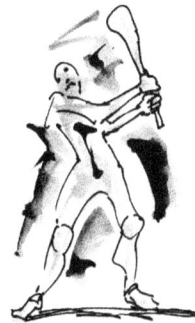

Your body may not be able to be in compliance with the code imposed upon you. OR your body will exceed the self-imposed limitations and you will break the code. This comes very dramatically into picture with illness. When one member of the family has an illness, others fear they may have it too, which is not necessary true. However, if they succumb to fear, they live in the code of expectation and limited belief that they cannot remain healthy.

Another example would be that parents assume their child is just as resilient as they are, when in fact he is very sensitive. The code they live by, could place this child in serious danger and jeopardy. Of course there is the factor of genetics, and inherited health challenges, as well as subtle body's memory of past trauma, that can be imprinted into the child's subtle body. However, the acquired codes are different, because they in fact do not agree with the physical state of your body, and perhaps even oppose it. It is not set in stone that you will inherit an illness, just as it is not logical that if your parents are healthy, you will be also.

YOU CARRY YOUR OWN INDIVIDUAL CODES THAT MAY SOMETIMES SERIOUSLY CLASH WITH CODES OF YOUR FAMILY, OR SOCIETY YOU LIVE IN.

Understanding that you are unique is of great importance. Accepting that your physical body is unique is as important. Developing self-awareness and attunement to your own individual physical qualities is as necessary as air. If you carry positive, empowering and healthy codes of physical self-awareness, strength, stamina, endurance and resilience, you will obviously have a considerably easier time navigating through life's possible challenges. PTSD can interfere with these naturally empowering codes and throw you off balance, preventing you from following your natural tendencies, desires and gifts. For example, an enthusiastic professional sportsman has an accident, and may suffer from considerable PTSD and fear of continuing to engage in the sport. This would be unfortunate. Overcoming PTSD associated with the accident will enable the sportsman to continue benefiting from naturally powerful codes that helped him pursue his desired sport.

In conclusion, the codes that affect your physical abilities and health are of great importance for obvious reasons. Recognizing the presence of negative codes in these areas is the first step to consciously dis-engage them and shift your belief system. Once this realization sets in, you will naturally want to distance yourself from anything that restrict or limits your true potential and desires.

> **THE CODES CAN BE OVERCOME WHEN YOU ARE AWARE OF THEM AND CONSCIOUSLY REALIZE HOW THEY LIMIT AND RESTRICT YOU.**

For example; if you realize that your health ailments do not have to be the same as of your family members, that you are your own person, and your physical needs and abilities may be significantly different from other people, then you allow yourself the possibility to enjoy limitless potential of health and physical stamina, perhaps even realizing your physical gifts and talents. This becomes a very empowering moment that can literally shift your life and help you fulfill the greatest potentials you have been naturally gifted with.

PTSD represents a potential for a glitch, a misstep, in causing your naturally given codes to stall and keep you stuck in fear. This healing journey is a reminder that your codes need to be observed, recognized, claimed, and used to your advantage, while striving for your highest evolutionary path. Develop a strong, confident, healthy, nurturing and physically resilient code in your core belief system, and begin acting with that intention and goal in mind. You are the only one that holds the power to reprogram your code the way you wish. Abandon all limitations and expand your mind.

YOUR CODE FOR LOVE AND RELATIONSHIPS

These codes are incredibly significant, as they practically determine how your partnerships and love-life will unfold, through the course of your life. Here we are talking about numerous aspects of your abilities, understanding, expectations and limited belief systems in regard to your behavior in relationships. This relates to many different kinds of relationships and basic human interaction patterns, whether with friends, coworkers, acquaintances, and of course your partners. The code of love that will significantly affect you is the code used by your parents – to you this may seem normal, acceptable and expectant. In previous chapter we learned of PTSD that may be associated with your childhood and how that affects your behavior later in life. I want to clarify that there is a difference between PTSD associated with childhood trauma, or your own relationship codes that represent a tainted or limited view of how relationships work. Childhood trauma associated with your parent's dysfunctional or traumatic behavior, left you with PTSD patterns. Codes are different from those patterns and represent your separate expectations and limited belief system as to what relationships are. While coming from a broken home may make it harder for you to imagine a happy marriage partnership, you may possess a code for happy and healthy relationship – your own coded belief system is intact and healthy. This will help you find, create and enjoy precisely that, regardless of how dysfunctional your parent's relationship model was.

YOUR PAST LIFE CODE WILL OVERRULE THE PTSD FROM YOUR CHILDHOOD.

You will endure the early turbulence and come out almost unscathed. With your deeper given understanding, your past life code will enable you to know that the dysfunctional relationship you may have witnessed up close, is not the only possible version of a partnership or marriage.

PTSD will affect you differently than a code. You may have in your subtle energy system codes for a most elevated, unconditional and loving partnership, yet have not ever seen it up close, witnessed it in others, or experienced it yourself – at least not in this lifetime – as of yet. But thanks to your code, you do know, that this kind of elevated relationship exists, and somewhere in you very distant memory, you carry a deep knowledge of how it feels when it's properly functioning. Until you find someone that fits within your past memory context of the best relationship dynamic code, you will feel something is amiss and not right. If your relationship code is limited and your expectations from a partner are thwarted by beliefs that don't make sense, or restrictive societal rules, you will feel pressured to follow these codes. Once you recognize your codes are limited, you will be able to consciously choose wether you will continue to follow them, or will explore the better, healthier, happier and optimal manifestation of love relationships. The next step becomes your exploration and learning process of how an optimal relationship unfolds, functions and sustains itself. Strive to develop a self-caring, loving, compassionate, respectful and giving relationship code in your core belief system, and begin acting with that intention and goal in mind. You are the only one that holds the power to reprogram your code the way you wish. Abandon all restrictive beliefs and expand your mind.

YOUR CODE FOR ABUNDANCE

This is certainly another incredibly interesting and existentially important aspect of your life. How do you relate to the possibility, reality, and proper ways of attaining and manifesting prosperity?

In the context of codes, it is very crucial how they have the potential to restrict or expand your possibilities to create and attract abundance into your life. In the case of restricting codes, you may believe that you do not have the ability to ascend higher and manifest any kind of extraordinary, or even just normal level of abundance, than your certain pre-conceived limitations indicate. An individual may be incredibly gifted and knowledgeable, but will never dare to pursue or even reveal all they could offer to the society. Someone else could easily attain a level of recognition or material reward for their natural gifts, but does not feel they can or should appear in public view. Another person may have an outstanding intellect and ability to create important discoveries, that may help large communities of people, yet they don't reveal them to anyone. They simply mistakenly believe that such a possibility is out of their reach. These people have codes that are afflicted and limiting, even obstructive.

On the other hand, you may have a person who doesn't seem to have much to offer, but they manage to courageously move forward and pursue the seemingly unattainable. No-one else around them attains any kind of prosperity, and yet, they easily tackle and turn everything they touch into gold and ascend way beyond what anyone expected. Perhaps they even become a beacon of hope for society, inspiring others and helping pave the way for big, transformative and uplifting change.

> **A PERSON MAY POSSESS A CODE THAT HELPS THEM EASILY OVERCOME THE OBVIOUS RESTRICTIONS AND LIMITATIONS IMPOSED UPON THEM WITHIN THEIR ORIGINAL, HUMBLE ENVIRONMENT.**

Despite all the odds, they manage to take their life into an entirely unexpected direction. No-one around them believed this was ever possible. And yet, here they are! This is a clear case of the person possessing strong codes which always helps them land on their feet, like a cat with nine lives. No matter where you place them, they manage to end up on top, strong, resilient and enduring. That is true abundance of Spirit, even if they are not materially wealthy, but simply maintain a principled and impactful life. We know that prosperity is not just material riches, certainly it can be, but what matters, is abundance in other areas, such as; contribution to the world and society, the ability to express compassion and help others in need, while enjoying a spirited fulfilling life, regardless the size of their bank account.

Where this situation relates to PTSD, is when for example; someone suffers the PTSD consequences that have traumatized and eliminated their belief and confidence factor. They may perpetually struggle in asserting their right to reasonable abundance and simple, basic levels of prosperity.

Remember, codes are past life belief systems that have no base in PTSD, negative or positive – in relation to prosperity. Review your codes of how you relate to and understand your engagement with prosperity, abundance, how your belief system restricts you and prevents you from prospering the way you could. Then ask yourself where this belief comes from. If you can't find it in your childhood, family, society, or immediate environment, then it's simply old, and it's time to release it, because it is not serving your best interest.

If you have the ease of way with abundance and feel you have mastered that aspect, then you are fortunate to have a well worked-out prosperity code that will assure your absolute abundance, no matter where you find yourself in this world, or what situations you face. This is important for you to examine. And again in relation to PTSD, you can consciously face the beliefs that have appeared as a result of a trauma and with awareness step by step diminish them.

STRIVE TO DEVELOP A SELF-CONFIDENT, ABUNDANT, COURAGEOUS, DISCIPLINED AND DISCERNING PROSPERITY CODE IN YOUR CORE - BELIEF SYSTEM.

Begin acting with that intention and goal in mind. You are the only one that holds the power to reprogram your code the way you wish. Abandon all past and expand your mind for an abundant present and future.

YOUR CODE FOR EMPOWERMENT

Finally, we arrive at the code that is a decisive navigator for your ability to make meaningful progress on your evolutionary path. Coming from a position of weakness, you are vulnerable to obvious traps of negative behavior in human nature, that brings us perhaps a period of temporary pleasure, but long lasting regret and suffering. Here we are talking about greed, and other fear-based acts that produce negative consequences. If your subtle body is permeated with codes that tend to steer you in the direction of weakness of human character, this will push you to assume there is nothing else, nothing better in life, there is no chance for you to rise above the circumstances you find yourself in, or a general sense of limitation and lack of choices. You are caught in a code that is like an energy draining vortex.

However, if your codes are of an empowering nature, you will always be able to navigate through the unknown, avoid dark corners and find your way out of the darkest of nights. You will use all your abilities to live by your truth, your principles, and overcome most impossible obstacles, always knowing in full awake consciousness what is the right way, and where you need to turn, to save yourself and others. In connection with PTSD effects of past trauma, that may have left you fearful to the extent of succumbing to life choices of lower frequency realms, you can transform your weak disposition with your own natural power codes that possess the positive information.

> **NO MATTER WHAT YOU HAVE ENDURED IN THIS LIFE,**
> **IF YOUR OLD CODE CARRIES A MESSAGE**
> **OF A NOBLE HEART AND ACTIONS,**
> **YOU SHALL ALWAYS PERSEVERE.**

If your code is weak in this area, and you feel doubtful of the goodness and the law of love, kindness, compassion and forgiveness, you will display weak choices in all areas of your life. Strive to develop a trust in divine power, the universal law of light above darkness, and the natural character empowerment code that resides in your core belief system.

Begin acting with that intention and goal in mind. You are the only one that holds the power to elevate your code the way you wish. Abandon all doubts, call your divine guides, expand your mind, and enter the field of endless possibilities.

YOUR ASSIGNMENT

AFFIRMATION

I AM REACTIVATING THE CODES FOR HEALTH, PROSPERITY AND LOVE WITHIN MY SUBTLE ENERGY BODY

DIARY

In this Chapter you became familiar with the incredible power of codes. Recognizing and activating your own power codes, should be your intention. At the same time, you can discover any limiting codes that are either your own, or clearly and easily identifiable through your childhood, family dynamics set-up, or social circumstance. This journey of code realignment is deeply healing and cleansing. Any old PTSD patterns will be overcome when your ancient positive power codes are recognized and reactivated. You will truly experience the shift of regaining control and power over your life, regardless of what you endured and how long your challenges persisted. Now you are free and ready to engage in your life in a whole new, yet familiarly healthy way.

PROCESS

Work thru the questions, come back in a few days, see if anything changed, add it on, clarify and self-discover through the process.

PRACTICE

This week is about fine tuning your expectations of what is possible, how your life becomes your opportunity to feature your gifts, enjoy your hard-earned blessings, and share your knowledge. You are special and no PTSD can erase all the wisdom gained from your past. Through your own empowerment codes you will realign and shift the dynamic. The time has come for you to shine. You deserve it, you want it, and you are ready for it.

YOUR EMPOWERMENT CODES ARE A SECRET RESERVOIR OF WISDOM.
OPEN THE DOOR AND ENTER.
YOU WILL TRANSFORM FROM WITHIN.

IDENTIFY YOUR CODES

1. WHAT IS YOUR CODE BELIEF ABOUT YOUR PHYSICAL ABILITY AND STRENGTH?

2. HOW DO YOU WISH TO IMPROVE THIS CODE?

3. WHAT IS YOUR CODE BELIEF ABOUT YOUR HEALTH?

4. HOW CAN YOU IMPROVE THIS CODE?

5. WHAT IS YOUR CODE BELIEF ABOUT YOUR FRIENDS?

6. WHAT IS YOUR CODE BELIEF ABOUT LOVE RELATIONSHIPS?

7. HOW DO YOU WISH TO IMPROVE THIS CODE?

8. WHAT IS YOUR CODE BELIEF ABOUT YOUR ABUNDANCE?

9. HOW DO YOU WISH TO IMPROVE THIS CODE?

10. WHAT IS YOUR CODE BELIEF ABOUT YOUR SUCCESS?

11. HOW DO YOU WISH TO IMPROVE THIS CODE?

12. WHAT IS YOUR CODE BELIEF FOR YOUR SELF-CONFIDENCE?

13. HOW DO YOU WISH TO IMPROVE THIS CODE?

14. WHAT IS YOUR CODE BELIEF ABOUT KARMA?

15. WHAT IS YOUR CODE BELIEF ABOUT GOD?

MUDRA FOR BALANCING YIN & YANG

Sit with a straight back and keep shoulders down, nice and relaxed. Connect the thumbs and index fingers, extending the rest of the fingers apart. Lift your right hand up in front of your chest with the palm turned outward, the fingertips pointing to the left. Hold the left hand below the right in front of your stomach area, palm turned inward and fingertips pointing to the right. Now connect the thumbs and index fingers of both hands, creating the Wheel of Life. Hold for Three minutes and relax.

BREATH
LONG, DEEP AND SLOW THRU YOUR NOSE

MANTRA
OMM *(God in His Absolute State)*

CHAKRAS
ALL CHAKRAS

HEALING COLORS
ALL COLORS

AFFIRMATION

I AM BALANCED IN MY HEART, MIND AND BODY

MUDRA for Universal Energy

Sit with a straight back, keep your shoulders down, nice and relaxed. Bend your elbows, bring your hands up and away from your body to form two V's. You can keep your arms slightly closer and lightly touching your body, to establish a stronger sense of powerful energy in your chest area, or leave some room between elbows and your body. Raise your palms to your heart level, keeping all fingers together. Feel the nurturing energy flowing into your hands. Hold for three minutes and relax.

BREATH
LONG, DEEP AND SLOW THRU YOUR NOSE

MANTRA
HAR HARE HAREE WAHE GURU
*(God, the Creator of Supreme Power and Wisdom,
the Spiritual Teacher and Guide Through Darkness)*

CHAKRAS
BASE OF SPINE - 1, CROWN - 7

HEALING COLORS
RED, VIOLET

AFFIRMATION

THE UNIVERSE IS MY ETERNAL LIFE SOURCE

MUDRA FOR POWERFUL INSIGHT

Sit with a straight back and keep your shoulders down, nice and relaxed. Bend your elbows and raise your hands to the level of the navel. Make a gentle fist with your left hand and place it palm facing up into the palm of your right hand. Left thumb tip is above the right. Concentrate on your Third Eye, breathe, and hold for three minutes.

BREATH

LONG, DEEP AND SLOW THRU YOUR NOSE

MANTRA

SAT NAM

(Truth is God's name, One in Spirit))

CHAKRA

THIRD EYE - 6

HEALING COLORS

INDIGO

AFFIRMATION

I CALL UPON MY INSIGHT AND DISCERNMENT

MUDRA for LOVE

Sit with a straight back and keep your shoulders down, nice and relaxed. Curl the middle and ring fingers into your palms and extend the index fingers and little fingers. Cross over the bent middle and ring fingers with your thumbs. Raise your arms up to the level of your head. Keep your elbows from sinking. Hold for Three minutes, then relax.

BREATH
INHALE EIGHT SHORT COUNTS, WITH ONE STRONG, LONG EXHALE

MANTRA
SAT NAM WAHE GURU
(God Is Truth, His Is the Supreme Power and Wisdom)

CHAKRA
HEART - 4

HEALING COLORS
GREEN & ROSE

AFFIRMATION

I BEAM LOVE AND AM ENVELOPED IN LIGHT

MUDRA FOR ATTRACTING ABUNDANCE

Sit with a straight back, keep your shoulders down, nice and relaxed. Lift the hands up, elbows bent, palms are at shoulder level, turned up towards the sky. Inhale and open the palms stretching all fingers. Hold for a few moments. Next, exhale and close your hands clasping them into firm but comfortable fists for a few moments. Repeat. Visualize the Universe's energy flowing into your hands and when closing hands, visualize capturing this abundant energy.

BREATH
LONG, DEEP AND SLOW THRU YOUR NOSE

MANTRA
SAT NAM *(Truth Is God's Name, One in Spirit)*

CHAKRAS
ALL CHAKRAS

HEALING COLORS
ALL COLORS

AFFIRMATION

I THRIVE, I DESERVE, I BELONG, I PROSPER

Week Eight

POSITIVE IMPACT~YOUR VICTORY

You are approaching the finish line of this healing and self-empowering journey. You explored the subtle intricate nuances and hidden elements of your PTSD challenges, and have awakened and thus began to mend all that needed your attention. Once you recognize and understand yourself, fearlessly examine the depths of your inner complexities, you are in the process of restoring the intricate fabric of your subtle body.

YOU CAN ONLY OVERCOME YOUR WEAKNESSES, IF AND WHEN YOU RECOGNIZE THEM.

You see, if you had a small boat and discovered there was a tiny leak somewhere, you simply couldn't ignore it. Instead, you'd embark on a search to find the tiny, hidden, but dangerous leak. Once you'd find it, you could fix it, and have it under control. You would keep checking every once in a while, to make sure that the repair still holds, but the leak would not continue to present the same challenge.

Similarly, the subtle energy consequences of PTSD are your energy leaks, that drain you of your valuable vital force. Once you find them, you can fix them, and nothing will catch you off guard again. You will remain self-aware, to make sure they never resurface. It will become a part of your maintenance program. From now on, you know enough to keep an eye out for the signs that cause you trouble. The weak spots, the emotional triggers and the fear-filled blocks are dissolved and healing. Now that you know all about them, you know they will drain you no more. Now my dear, you are in the clear and your power is restored.

YOUR GAINED WISDOM

This is the time to gather what you gained through all your experiences and count the great golden nuggets. PTSD is always associated with challenging, difficult, disruptive and unpleasant happenings and experiences in one's life – for obvious reasons. However, once the initial trauma has passed and the healing process takes place, there are numerous positive outcomes while you navigate through this journey. One of them is, to always seek and find positive aspects and realizations acquired through each challenge you experienced.

And while this may seem difficult at times, when you gain some distance from the raw traumatic events, you rapidly enter an entirely different stage of relating to your past. You unveiled and uncover some things and begin to understand the bigger picture. Somehow you actually find hidden treasures, stemming from the entire difficult journey.

The treasures are your firsthand experience and profoundly deep understanding of the complex situations that you lived through. You have a unique knowledge how such situations occur, how it feels to be personally involved, seemingly helpless while caught in dramatic scope of events.

> ## PROCESSING YOUR PTSD OFFERS YOU VALUABLE WISDOM
> ## AND OPENS UP NEW, POSITIVE OPPORTUNITIES,
> ## THAT YOU NEVER EXPECTED.

First-hand experience of various traumas may momentarily overwhelm you, but later, it can truly empower you and evoke hope. It may even propel a great positive change, and perhaps a significant shift in your life's path and mission. The healing process can be lengthy and tedious, old wounds may reopen, prior unresolved issues can escalate before they finally subside and leave, resolved once and for all. You will recognize patterns, and similarities that will help you understand why and how you found yourself in such a challenged situation. The process is different for each one of us, since our lives are unique and our perceptions, sensitivities, strengths and weaknesses come in countless combinations.

For example, in PTSD related to grief, which is a deeply personal experience and completely unique to each one of us, there are no rules how long or how intensely one shall grieve. Similarly, there are no rules how long one should experience the various levels and challenging PTSD manifestations as consequences of trauma. Time works differently for each one of us. What matters is that you allow yourself to feel, process, and reconstruct a new inner balance to help you alleviate all pressure to overcome the PTSD as fast as possible. When you take your time and respect each emotion that surfaces, you are cleansing your energy field systematically, patiently, and with a clear purpose. During this entire process your uniquely gained wisdom will crystalize, and you will be amazed at all you've gained. Yes, it was painful, but your wisdom is valuable beyond measure. It presents an interesting part of the puzzle describing your ever-important life's journey and mission.

YOUR HIGHER PURPOSE

Many of us spend years wondering and seeking for an answer to this particular question. When we journey through our unique life experiences, we understand that in fact there is no absolutely written-in-stone scenario. There is flexibility, there are numerous possible storylines, options, choices, and there are certainly consequences. Our decisions help us move forward on our path and find answers to questions that haunt and inspire us.

Your higher purpose may seem clear to you at a particular point in your life, perhaps even early on in your life. It may be something others simply expect of you, it may be a very ordinary life, or it may be unusual, not the norm, and simply different from others. While you learn your lessons, overcome your struggles, lose and win your battles, you eventually get wounded, like any stoic warrior would. It's all part of life, and you can't expect to move through fire unscathed. But when you come out on the other side, you are transformed and your perception of reality is altered. After some time of healing, you are granted revelations, realizations and spiritual awakenings. You begin to understand step by step or…in a momentary epiphany, precisely what you've always wondered about. You begin to recognize your higher purpose.

This is when challenges turn into blessings. This is the moment when everything begins to make sense and you see the bigger picture, the perfectly destined path that you had to undertake in order to land where you are now. I don't mean to suggest that you have to necessarily go through a heavy traumatic experience in order to recognize your higher purpose. But you do have to learn. And the lessons come and manifest in unexpected ways.

**WE ALL HAVE TO LEARN LIFE'S LESSONS.
JUST LIKE THERE IS NO PROPER MEASURE FOR GRIEF,
THERE IS NO PROPER MEASURE FOR TRAUMA.**

Our experiences can be compared, but they cannot be measured. How do you measure sadness or happiness? It is immeasurable. How you reemerge and come out at the other end, is all that matters.

WE EACH HAVE DIFFERENT LEVELS OF RESILIENCE. A SEEMINGLY SMALL TRAUMA FOR YOU, MAY BE GIGANTIC OR INSURMOUNTABLE FOR SOMEONE ELSE.

So in that context, we each have to endure learning experiences which may not always be pleasant, because life is simply not made from only pleasant experiences. If you do not know the darkness you won't appreciate the light, in fact, if you had non-stop light you may begin to dislike it. Or at the least you would take it for granted and not appreciate it. There is a fine balance in life that we all need to find and cultivate. The revelation of higher purpose will affect the way you perceive love, relationships, success, life and death and every tiny aspect of your human experience. It is like you are walking on a path through a forest. If you don't know where you are going, it may seem a bit unsettling, nerve wrecking, even adventurous, but not something you'd want to continue indefinitely. Eventually, you'd like to settle down and have some inner peace and know where you are going. An excursion that began as an adventure can quickly become tiresome and undesirable, when you're living in the dark. This is in stark contrast to actually knowing your destination and your mission, while you are journeying through life. Each step suddenly becomes purposeful, meaningful and intentional. This permeates your life with a very different energy. As a consequence, each action you perform with clarity of intention shall be received accordingly. It is truly like night and day, two entirely different experiences. Knowing your higher purpose is about knowing why you are here and what is your mission. Loaded with this crucial information makes every new moment coming your way filled with deep awareness, and conscious presence.

THE BLESSING OF KNOWING YOUR HIGHER PURPOSE IS SATURATED WITH POTENTIAL TO SUCCESSFULLY FULFILL YOUR MISSION.

Your traumatic experience and your brave and intentional healing process of working through it, will gift you with clarity and realization of how you can contribute to the betterment of this world. This will undoubtedly reveal an intricate part of your higher purpose. Once you possess that knowledge, you hold in your hands all needed tools to make this life as fulfilled, impactful, noble and spiritually evolved as possible.

YOUR UNUSUAL ABILITIES

Your past life experiences leave you with another golden nugget, a special gift. You have acquired a specialized ability to understand a complex situation, that you experienced from a very unique and real-life perspective. A person may make an effort in explaining to others how something should feel and look like, but it is an entirely different thing, if they have actually experienced it and can explain it in a very real and tangible way, so that everyone can truly understand it.

But more than that, when you gain unusual abilities and knowledge, you are in a very unique position to help others. This becomes a choice, for you are not obliged to revisit your traumatic experience and gained knowledge. But often you will choose and feel a need to share some specific unique aspects of your past, that could be of incredible importance and help to others.

> **YOUR KNOWLEDGE OF A SPECIFIC TRAUMA, COULD OFFER OTHERS A LIFELINE TO HELP SAVE THEMSELVES, OR SPARE THEM YEARS OF AGONY TRYING TO FIGURE SOMETHING OUT.**

You can help them endure and resiliently overcome a similar challenge they may be facing. After all, just think about the fact, that all the knowledge shared had to be gained somewhere, somehow. It's quite amazing to reflect upon all the trials and tribulations that people endured, in order to leave behind the knowledge and information we have now, at our fingertips. But there is another aspect that may be very beneficial to you. While you experienced your challenges, you could discover some untapped and unknown special abilities and gifts that you possessed that you would otherwise never even know about.

For example; if the traumatic experience pushed you into a situation that was difficult to sustain and you had to find a way out, or had to invent an innovative, self-preserving way that helped you survive, you now possess this knowledge. When we find ourselves in pressing situations, survival instinct kicks-in with great power. As a direct result, you may come upon a great breakthrough that will later help others. Your experience may even trigger within you a new resolve in regard to your life mission, your career path, your volunteer activities, and creative projects.

WHEN WE FEEL INTENSE EMOTIONS, WE ARE TRANSFORMED.

Of course it is preferable that the emotions are pleasant, but emotions of suffering often unleash the greatest creative potential. Just think of how many passionate songs were written during a traumatic heartbreak. Once people are happy they seem incapable of writing heart wrenching passionate music, or at least it is not intertwined with a do-or-die passion. This is sometimes the greatest challenge for artists, because once they succeed, the survival misery and struggle is over and they find themselves empty and void of passionate creative force. In desperation, they get lost in abusing mind altering substances, while trying to reach that creative source that was open while they were in turmoil. Now they find themselves in a different turmoil, and certainly not a creative one.

Creativity does not have to stem from suffering, but is a highly healing technique to endure through it. If one is in emotional pain, creativity can be a healing outlet. When one is carefree and happy, they usually prefer to enjoy life and not pour their heart out. However, you can be immensely creative without any suffering, but the results will be colored with different kinds of emotions.

ANYTHING GAINED FROM YOUR TRAUMATIC EXPERIENCE REMAINS A PART OF YOU. IT IS UP TO YOU, TO TURN IT INTO AN ASSET.

Your special gifts, knowledge gained and unusual abilities revealed as a result of past trauma are your hidden gifts. Are you aware of them and can you put them to use?
If you've endured a challenging and traumatic event in your life, what special ability helped you survive?

Perhaps you can intertwine it into your life mission. Think about it, reflect upon it, and see if anything of your knowledge gained could be useful to others and would be a pleasure to share. If your knowledge gained is of more private nature and you don't feel comfortable sharing it directly, find a more indirect way. You'll figure it out. The most important thing is that you become aware of it and have a choice of how you'd like to share it with others.

Why should you share it? Because that way, you did not suffer in vain. And this can be a great consolation to help you overcome any sense of bitterness, victimhood or helplessness.

YOU ARE IN CHARGE WHAT YOU DO WITH YOUR LIFE'S KNOWLEDGE. PUT IT TO BEST USE POSSIBLE.

YOUR DEEPER UNDERSTANDING

This is another dimension of your growing process. We are not talking about the light-weight, outer realization, but about the awakened awareness of a deeper meaning of life, your purpose and life's mission. Dramatic experiences make us reevaluate life in general. Perhaps we suddenly value life much more than we ever did. If we came close to death, this was a major turning point.

For example; someone who had a close brush with death due to careless, reckless, self-destructive behavior, will after a fortunate "escape" value their life in an entirely new way. They understand and realize that a second chance has been given to them and will probably never repeat the prior mistakes. We usually have a tendency to take for granted what is given to us, and realize its value if or when it's taken away. If your health is challenged, you will hopefully make a big turnabout and begin taking care of your body. If your relationship came close to being lost, you will now make an effort to preserve it. If your family member was in danger, you will suddenly love them even more. When someone or something you were taking for granted was almost lost, the traumatic experience will instantly awaken a deep realization and clarity of your life's true priorities.

And finally, the deeper understanding of what truly matters in life, what is the most important principle, action, or a person that matters most, will shift your entire perspective. You will gain clarity of what is something worth preserving, sacrificing for, and tolerating, in order to sustain and nurture it in your life. It is unfortunate that we often don't appreciate various persons or circumstances until they are gone or close to it. But such is human nature.

HEALING A TRAUMATIC EXPERIENCE WILL HELP YOU BECOME CRYSTAL CLEAR ABOUT WHAT MATTERS TO YOU MOST AND WHY YOU ARE HERE.

Your deeper understanding will transform the way you relate to people, and all of your past, present and future life experiences from here on. In addition, you will experience enlightened clarity as it relates to this material world, all things that perish and what remains when all is lost.

Love comes in many different manifestations, but its essence is unmistakable. And love is indestructible, for it goes on beyond the limitations of space and time. Love is untouchable by death or physical departure. Once you truly understand and embrace this realization, you will shift everything in your daily life. The way you relate to others, the way you spend your days and the way you communicate – if you know that all that really matters is to experience love, you will live according to those principles and not waste any time bickering, complaining and feeling sorry for yourself.

You will move on and make every effort to sustain, attract and protect the love in your life that you have. If love seems to elude you, then your lesson is to open up and allow the Universal love into your life, introducing people, opportunities and activities that will help open your heart. You will experience the ultimate Universal emotion that can uplift any human. Remember, your natural frequency is at your optimal capacity when you are filled with love. Wouldn't you want to function at your highest level all the time?

YOUR CHANCE TO GUIDE

If you were stuck in a dark tunnel that you traveled before, you would know the way out. Next time you'll take that journey and meet a few lost people that are exhausted and filled with tangible fear, you will help them tag along, and show them a way out of the maze.
Why? Because it is your human duty to be kind and helpful to all in need. Especially if you possess the knowledge that may eliminate another person's suffering. Someone has to be the first to go through the dark tunnel. Someone has to be the first to find a solution to a challenge. And sometimes you are that someone special that discovers an answer that saves you and others.

**SHARING KNOWLEDGE THAT ALLEVIATES SUFFERING
IS YOUR PRIVILEGE, CONTRIBUTION AND DUTY.**

It creates an ideal opportunity to display and practice acts of a generous spirit, kindness, compassion, generosity and …love. Guiding others is a privilege, but do keep in mind that it will produce the most fruitful results when and if you are asked to do so. If a person needs you and says so, asks for help or guidance, then your actions will be appreciated. You need to learn to discern who truly needs your help and who is only asking of you to sustain and facilitate their dysfunction, laziness or sense of entitlement.

This presents another lesson in discernment – for you. It is a very important one, for if you cannot wisely choose who you shall help but give pearls to ones who are not receptive, you will learn another unpleasant lesson. Life will test you how generous you are, how gullible, and how well you are able to discern. Giving and guiding others is a tremendous honor, and a gift in itself. It offers new learning experiences for you to develop further and give even more. Give to all who ask and deserve and see the pain of your past transform into a most beautiful opportunity for multiplying happiness of today.

YOUR OPPORTUNITY TO CREATE CHANGE

E very time you allow for a positive shift of your consciousness, you are open and willing to flow with the change at hand. This ability is a tremendous gift, for it takes you to the highest potentials of your life. When you change, others are affected and more change follows. It is like a ripple effect throughout the Universe. It spreads and gains in velocity and power. If your change is of a positive nature, others are affected in even more positive ways. It's like you turn the tide. I know that often we can feel helpless, especially when surrounded by turmoil and hardship, pushing so many to the limits. But no matter what challenges or circumstances you find yourself in, you have the ability to sustain your inner calm. Yes, the upheaval will affect you, but it won't topple you over. You are resilient, you have stamina, and past experiences that made you even stronger, more assured and confident of your path.

FORWARD, ALWAYS STRIVE TO MOVE FORWARD, TOWARDS THE LIGHT. THIS IS OF HIGHEST IMPORTANCE AND GREATEST VALUE.

This way, you will be able to overcome any challenge and sustain your inner resolve to journey through life victoriously, with dignity, in kindness to others while using your treasure chest of hard-earned knowledge, which is unique and helpful to all in need. You are traveling on the very edge of the most powerful change, the fight for the Light. Your words, actions and pursuits matter more than you know. Remain steady and secure, determined to see your mission through.

YOUR ASSIGNMENT

AFFIRMATION

> ### MY SACRED KNOWLEDGE IS OVERFLOWING,
> ### MY POWER IS INDESTRUCTIBLE

DIARY

In this Chapter you are recognizing and collecting all your hard-earned rewards that you gained through your challenging experiences. All difficulties bring us some wisdom, knowledge and resilience. Recognizing this will magnify the positive after-effects. Ignorance creates an even bigger loss than you already suffered. It is an intricate part of life to have the ability to bounce-back, remain optimistic, enthusiastic and hopeful for all possibilities to remain open, and full of wonderful potential.

This is what makes the biggest difference in the sum of all experiences, lessons and adventures we live through. Understanding that we must expect goodness, as it will bring more goodness into our life. If you live in fear of repeating or experiencing any pain from your past, you are blocking new positive, rewarding and wonderful experiences from entering your life.

On subtle energy level, when finding and seeing the positive, you will attract more of it. When fearing the bad, your vibration descends and is less able to attract and receive the positive. Therefore consciously keep your frequency up with a calm, open disposition. Trust the Universe in knowing, that it will always bring you protection, joy and precisely what is in your very best interest. Your journey is unique, cannot be compared to others, and has a one of-a-kind assignment.

PROCESS

Work thru the questions, come back in a few days, see if anything changed, add it on, clarify and self-discover through the process.

PRACTICE

This is our final week of intensive re-programming study to conquer PTSD and consciously triumph over any lingering undesirable remains. Now, you have lightened your load substantially, and replaced the darkness with light, the sorrow with peace, and the fear with love.

You are ready to become the beacon of Light.
If you can help and are asked to do so, you should.
If you prefer to help in more invisible ways, you can.
If you find a creative outlet to continue your healing process, go on.
If you wish to change the world, do so.

Remember, every kind word creates a ripple effect of kindness and hope.
And hope is as necessary as air, the sun and love.
Carry on, for now you are the messenger of Light.

> ## THE JOURNEY OF LIFE HAS UNEXPECTED TURNS AND HIDDEN TREASURES. UNCOVER YOURS DAILY.

IN CONCLUSION

This is the final set of Mudras for your healing journey. Hopefully you have found your favorite ones, and have established a regular, daily Mudra practice.

When you travel through your future adventures, stay connected to Mudras with your heart. Always remain sensitive and in-tune with their powerfully beneficial effects. With time, they will only gain in power.

Enjoy this ancient treasure and always allow sufficient time for healing energy to fully permeate your physical and subtle body. Soak it up and thrive!

RECOGNIZE YOUR GAINS AND TRIUMPHS

1. WHAT WISDOM DID YOU GAIN THROUGH YOUR CHALLENGING EXPERIENCES?

2. HOW HAS YOUR HIGHER PURPOSE CRYSTALIZED AS A RESULT OF THIS?

3. WHAT UNUSUAL ABILITIES DO YOU NOW HAVE, AS A RESULT OF YOUR PAST?

4. DID YOU GAIN A DEEPER UNDERSTANDING?

5. DO YOU SEE AN OPPORTUNITY TO HELP GUIDE OTHERS?

6. HOW CAN YOUR NEW AWARENESS HELP CREATE CHANGE?

7. CAN YOU HELP LEAD OTHERS OUT OF DARKNESS, PAIN, CONFUSION, GRIEF AND LOSS?

8. HOW CAN YOU INSPIRE OTHERS?

9. WHAT IS YOUR NEWFOUND PURPOSE AFTER THIS JOURNEY?

10. WRITE YOUR OWN WISDOM QUOTE:

MUDRA FOR NURTURING YOUR HEART

Sit with a straight back and keep your shoulders down, nice and relaxed. Connect the index and thumb fingertips, the rest of the fingers remain straight. Now place the right hand over your heart, left side of your chest and the left hand crossing over the right, touching the right side of your chest. Hands are resting on your chest, middle, ring and little fingers are kept straight. Feel the soothing, nurturing energy enter your heart and chest area.

BREATH

LONG, DEEP AND SLOW THRU YOUR NOSE

MANTRA

OMM *(God in His Absolute State)*

CHAKRA

HEART - 4

HEALING COLORS

GREEN & ROSE

AFFIRMATION

MY HEART IS OVERFLOWING WITH LOVE

MUDRA FOR CALMING YOUR MIND

Sit with a straight back, shoulders down, nice and relaxed. Cross your arms in front of your chest, elbows bent at a ninety-degree angle. Arms are parallel to the ground. The right hand is on top of the left arm and left hand below the right arm. All fingers are together and straight. Keep your elbows from sinking. Hold for Three minutes, then relax and be still.

BREATH
LONG, DEEP AND SLOW THRU YOUR NOSE

MANTRA
OM (*God in his absolute state*)

CHAKRAS
SOLAR PLEXUS -3. CROWN - 7

HEALING COLORS
YELLOW, VIOLET

AFFIRMATION

I AM SERENE AND COMPOSED

MUDRA for Illuminating Your HEART

Sit with a straight back and keep your shoulders down, nice and relaxed. Cross the hands in front of your heart, right hand over left. Left palm is closest to your body. Both palms are turned towards your chest. Gently connect the extended thumbs lengthwise, hook them together and point them upwards. All fingers are straight, right small finger is held apart. Hold for Three minutes and relax.

BREATH
LONG, DEEP AND SLOW THRU YOUR NOSE
MANTRA
OMM *(God in His Absolute State)*
CHAKRA
HEART - 4, CROWN - 7
HEALING COLORS
GREEN & ROSE, VIOLET
AFFIRMATION

I AM A BEACON OF LIGHT

MUDRA for EMPOWERING Your VOICE

Sit with a straight back, shoulders down, nice and relaxed. Bend your elbows and hold them parallel to the ground as you bring your hands up in front of you, at the level of your throat. Turn the right palm outward and the left palm toward you. Now bend your fingers and hook your hands together, the left hand on the outside. Gently pull on the hands as if trying to pull them apart, while keeping your shoulders down. Hold for Three minutes, then relax.

BREATH
LONG, DEEP AND SLOW THRU YOUR NOSE

CHAKRA
THROAT - 5

HEALING COLOR
BLUE

AFFIRMATION

MY WORDS INSPIRE, MOTIVATE AND CELEBRATE

MUDRA for VICTORY

Sit with a straight back and keep your shoulders down, nice and relaxed. Make gentle fists with both hands. Lift up your arms and cross them over your upper chest, left over right. This powerful Mudra is seen in many sculptures of Egyptian Pharaohs. Practice for Three minutes, then relax.

BREATH
LONG, DEEP AND SLOW THRU YOUR NOSE
MANTRA
OMM *(God in His Absolute State)*
CHAKRAS
ALL CHAKRAS
HEALING COLORS
ALL COLORS
AFFIRMATION

I AM VICTORIOUS AND SUCCESSFUL

MUDRA FOR AWAKENING YOUR DIVINE POTENTIAL

Sit with a straight back and keep your shoulders down, nice and relaxed. Make gentle fists with your hands and stretch out your thumbs. Bend your elbows, lift up your arms in front of your chest and press your forearms together all the way from your elbows to your wrists. The knuckles and thumbs of both hands are touching, thumbs are pointing up towards the sky. Hold for Three minutes and relax.

BREATH
LONG, DEEP AND SLOW THRU YOUR NOSE
MANTRA
OMM *(God in His Absolute State)*
CHAKRAS
ALL CHAKRAS
HEALING COLORS
ALL COLORS
AFFIRMATION

I AWAKEN MY OPTIMAL DIVINE POTENTIAL

YOUR MOMENT TO LEAD AND INSPIRE

When your life presented you with seemingly insurmountable challenges, you persevered. You didn't just survive, but you managed to overcome, move on, and uplift yourself out of the ashes like a phoenix, never to be brought down by flames.

This is inspiring. When we see someone overcome and triumph, we are in awe. If we had a similar challenge, but are still struggling to move past it, this kind of story gives us hope.

You can offer hope to others. You can help them overcome whatever they are going through, offer them the possibility to see a new, healthy and empowered way of life, untainted by the past and open to the endless possibilities of their future.

You see, your battleground can turn into an exemplary platform, that brings a lot of goodness. Even if you keep a low profile, you can use your knowledge and awareness through various kinds of contributions to this world.

However you choose to use your exemplary surviving spirit, you have the chance to shine and lead others through their turmoil. You can show them that each setback, battle and struggle offers you the ultimate triumph over trauma, and a new chance to experience a happy, fulfilling and most meaningful life.

Your moment to shine is here. Your time to inspire others has arrived.

And if your heart tells you so, you may lead them to remember that they too have the ability to shine, inspire and lead those that come behind them. So, I encourage you to recognize how blessed and lucky we all are, when a challenge presents itself on our life's path.

It is really an opportunity in disguise, prompting you to fight, struggle and eventually recognize in celebration your brave and shining spirit, that is traveling through this human life experience with such courage, bravery and resolve. You are an inspiration, you are blessed and you shall always triumph. May the Universe bless you today and every day forward, forever more.
You hold the Light.

Sabrina

MUDRA INDEX

ABOUT THE AUTHOR

SABRINA MESKO Ph.D.H. is a recognized Mudra authority and International and Los Angeles Times bestselling author of the timeless classic *Healing Mudras - Yoga for your Hands* translated into fourteen languages. She authored over twenty books on Mudras, Mudra Therapy, Mudras and Astrology, Meditation techniques, Spirituality and Holistic Care.

Sabrina was born in Europe where she became a classical ballerina at an early age. In her teens she moved to New York and became a principal Broadway dancer and singer who turned to yoga to heal a back injury. Eastern-trained but Western-based, she completed a several-year intensive study of teachings with world renowned Masters, one of whom entrusted her with bringing the sacred Mudra techniques to the West. She is a Yoga College of India certified Yoga Therapist.

Sabrina holds a Bachelors Degree in Sensory Approaches to Healing, a Masters in Holistic Science, and a Doctorate in Ancient and Modern Approaches to Healing from the American Institute of Holistic Theology. She is board certified from the American Alternative medical Association and American Holistic Health Association.

She has been featured in media outlets such as The Los Angeles Times, CNBC News, Cosmopolitan, the cover of London Times Lifestyle, The Discovery Channel documentary on Hands, W magazine, First for Women, Health, Web-MD, Daily News, Focus, Yoga Journal, Australian Women's weekly, Blend, Daily Breeze, New Age, the Roseanne Show and various international live television programs. Her articles have been published in world-wide publications. She hosted her own weekly TV show educating about health, well-being and complementary medicine. She is an executive member of the World Yoga Council and has led numerous international Yoga Therapy educational programs. She directed and produced her interactive double DVD titled *Chakra Mudras,* a Visionary Awards finalist. Sabrina also created award winning international Spa and Wellness Centers and is a motivational keynote conference speaker addressing large audiences all over the world. Sabrina recently launched Arnica Press, a boutique Book Publishing House. Her mission is to discover, mentor, nurture and publish unique authors with a meaningful message, that may otherwise not have an opportunity to be heard.

She is the founder of MUDRA MASTERY ™ the world's only online Mudra Teacher and Mudra Therapy Education, Certification, and Mentorship program, with her certified graduates and therapists spreading these ancient teachings in over 26 countries around the world.

WWW.SABRINAMESKO.COM

www.ingramcontent.com/pod-product-compliance
Lightning Source LLC
Chambersburg PA
CBHW081151270326
41930CB00014B/3117